Subject and Agency in Psychoanalysis

PSYCHOANALYTIC CROSSCURRENTS
General Editor: Leo Goldberger

SUBJECT AND AGENCY IN PSYCHOANALYSIS

Which Is to Be Master?

Frances M. Moran

NEW YORK UNIVERSITY PRESS
New York and London

NEW YORK UNIVERSITY PRESS
New York and London

Library of Congress Cataloging-in-Publication Data
Moran, Frances M.
Subject and agency in psychoanalysis : which is to be master? /
Frances M. Moran.
p.   cm. — (Psychoanalytic crosscurrents)
Includes bibliographical references and index.
ISBN 0-8147-5482-1
1. Psychoanalysis—Philosophy—History.   2. Self—Philosophy—
History.   3. Will—Philosophy—History.   4. Freud, Sigmund,
1856–1939. I. Title. II. Series.
[DNLM: 1. Psychoanalytic Theory.   2. Self Concept.   WM 460.5.E3
M829s]
BF175.M67   1993
150.19'52—dc20
DNLM/DLC
for Library of Congress   92-48288
CIP

Manufactured in the United States of America

c 10 9 8 7 6 5 4 3 2 1

Because of Peter William Musgrave

"When *I* use a word," Humpty Dumpty said in rather a scornful tone, "it means just what I choose it to mean—neither more nor less."

"The question is," said Alice, "whether you *can* make words mean different things."

"The question is," said Humpty Dumpty, "which is to be master—that's all."

—Lewis Carroll, *Through the Looking-Glass and What Alice Found There*

Contents

A Proposed Solution

Diagrams

Foreword

The *Psychoanalytic Crosscurrents* series presents selected books and monographs that reveal the growing intellectual ferment within and across the boundaries of psychoanalysis.

Freud's theories and grand-scale speculative leaps have been found wanting, if not disturbing, from the very beginning and have led to a succession of derisive attacks, shifts in emphasis, revisions, modifications, and extensions. Despite the chronic and, at times, fierce debate that has characterized psychoanalysis, not only as a movement but also as a science, Freud's genius and transformational impact on the twentieth century have never been seriously questioned. Recent psychoanalytic thought has been subjected to dramatic reassessments under the sway of contemporary currents in the history of ideas, philosophy of science, epistemology, structuralism, critical theory, semantics, and semiology as well as in sociobiology, ethology, and neurocognitive science. Not only is Freud's place in intellectual history being meticulously scrutinized, but his texts, too, are being carefully read, explicated, and debated within a variety of conceptual frameworks and sociopolitical contexts.

The legacy of Freud is perhaps most notably evident within the narrow confines of psychoanalysis itself, the "impossible profession" that has served as the central platform for the promulgation of official orthodoxy. But Freud's contributions—his original radical thrust—reach far beyond the parochial concerns of the clinician psychoanalyst as clinician. His writings touch on a wealth of issues, crossing traditional boundaries—be they situated in the biological, social, or humanistic spheres—that have profoundly altered our conception of the individual and society.

xiii

A rich and flowering literature, falling under the rubric of "applied psychoanalysis," came into being, reached its zenith many decades ago, and then almost vanished. Early contributors to this literature, in addition to Freud himself, came from a wide range of backgrounds both within and outside the medical/psychiatric field, and many later became psychoanalysts themselves. These early efforts were characteristically reductionist in their attempt to extrapolate from psychoanalytic theory (often the purely clinical theory) to explanation of phenomena lying at some distance from the clinical. Over the years, academic psychologists, educators, anthropologists, sociologists, political scientists, philosophers, jurists, literary critics, art historians, artists, and writers, among others (with or without formal psychoanalytic training), have joined in the proliferation of this literature.

The intent of the *Psychoanalytic Crosscurrents* series is to apply psychoanalytic ideas to topics that may lie beyond the narrowly clinical, but its essential conception and scope are quite different. The present series eschews the reductionist tendency to be found in much traditional "applied psychoanalysis." It acknowledges not only the complexity of psychological phenomena but also the way in which they are embedded in social and scientific contexts that are constantly changing. It calls for a dialectical relationship to earlier theoretical views and conceptions rather than a mechanical repetition of Freud's dated thoughts. The series affirms the fact that contributions to and about psychoanalysis have come from many directions. It is designed as a forum for the multidisciplinary studies that intersect with psychoanalytic thought but without the requirement that psychoanalysis necessarily be the starting point or, indeed, the center focus. The criteria for inclusion in the series are that the work be significantly informed by psychoanalytic thought or that it be aimed at furthering our understanding of psychoanalysis in its broadest meaning as theory, practice, and sociocultural phenomenon; that it be of current topical interest and that it provide the critical reader with contemporary insights; and, above all, that it be high-quality scholarship, free of absolute dogma, banalization, and empty jargon. The author's professional identity and particular theoretical orientation matter only to the extent that such facts may serve to frame the work for the reader, alerting him or her to inevitable biases of the author.

The *Psychoanalytic Crosscurrents* series presents an array of works from the multidisciplinary domain in an attempt to capture the ferment of scholarly activities at the core as well as at the boundaries of psychoanalysis. The books and monographs are from a variety of sources: authors will be psychoanalysts—traditional, neo- and post-Freudian, existential, object relational, Kohutian, Lacanian, etc.—social scientists with quantitative or qualitative orientations to psychoanalytic data, and scholars from the vast diversity of approaches and interests that make up the humanities. The series entertains works on critical comparisons of psychoanalytic theories and concepts as well as philosophical examinations of fundamental assumptions and epistemic claims that furnish the base for psychoanalytic hypotheses. It includes studies of psychoanalysis as literature (discourse and narrative theory) as well as the application of psychoanalytic concepts to literary criticism. It will serve as an outlet for psychoanalytic studies of creativity and the arts. Works in the cognitive and the neurosciences will be included to the extent that they address some fundamental psychoanalytic tenet, such as the role of dreaming and other forms of unconscious mental processes.

It should be obvious that an exhaustive enumeration of the types of works that might fit into the *Psychoanalytic Crosscurrents* series is pointless. The studies comprise a lively and growing literature as a unique domain; books of this sort are frequently difficult to classify or catalog. Suffice it to say that the overriding aim of the editor of this series is to serve as a conduit for the identification of the outstanding yield of that emergent literature and to foster its further unhampered growth.

Leo Goldberger
Professor of Psychology
New York University

Subject and Agency in Psychoanalysis

Introduction: The Question Asked

Truly fruitful research requires a twofold ability in its initial stage: first, the ability to ask the right question and, second, the ability to ask this question within the right framework. Failure to formulate the question correctly or failure to pose it within the most appropriate framework leads to problems at both a theoretical and a practical level. Perhaps this point can best be illustrated by my recounting my own search for an answer to a question concerning the notion of "self."

As I remember it now, my search began, at least at some level, when I was an adolescent. Like my friends at the time, I was asking the then-unformulated question "Who am I?" I suppose, in retrospect, that I was undergoing what might be termed the typical Ericksonian identity crisis even though I was unaware of anything more than a series of partially articulated queries about myself, others, and the world in which I lived. It is these very same queries that have given impetus to numerous attempts to search for answers over a period spanning many years. It is probable that many people ask self-related questions at varying stages of their existence. Whether or not they engage themselves seriously in the pursuit of answers to their questions is perhaps an indication of the intensity and urgency with which the questions are asked. In my own case a seemingly insatiable self-interrogation has in some sense pursued me, and I have made various attempts—some more serious than others—to deal with it. On numerous occasions I have fallen prey to time-consuming introspection in the hope of understanding myself. Dependent on my life circumstances, this introspection has been informed by either philosophical or metaphysical notions. Needless to say, like David Hume[1] and

Henri-Fréderic Amiel,[2] I found that my self-interrogation proved to be unsatisfying. In effect, I was led no further than to the point of an infinite regression, for who was the self that conducted the act of introspection? The continual failure of this method of investigation resulted in my asking self-related questions within the academic arena of scientific psychology. Somehow I had imagined that within this field I might find a more rigorous and trustworthy approach to cope with my undisciplined self-related search—one that might well be recognized by some as no more than a Franklian-like[3] search for meaning. I had hoped that the demands of the scientific paradigm would produce a discipline of mind that would enable me to explore productively the issues related to my self-interrogation. Thus, I could be relieved from my growing sense of doubt in regard to the possibility of gaining some type of valid self-knowledge.

As an honors thesis within the School of Behavioural Sciences at La Trobe University (Melbourne), I explored an aspect of the self-concept self-esteem, because it seemed to me that this notion might have potential as an explanatory concept in relation to one's behavior. I later worked on a Master's thesis within a Professional Course for Clinical Psychology at the University of Melbourne, where I investigated a developmental approach to the concept of self. Both these theses were undertaken within the context of the statistical-experimental approach of contemporary research. The result of the combined efforts, in terms of my self-related search, was insignificant when compared with the time and effort involved in their presentation. In sum, I was disillusioned with the potential of scientific psychology to give me the answers to the self-referential questions that I continued to ask. I was no nearer understanding what was meant by the term *self* than I had been following my prior attempted introspection. However, what I did gain from these academic exercises was a crystallization or clarification of the nature of my basic question. Through the process of trying to ground my ideas in testable theoretical formulations, I was able to distill the form of the question that continued to remain unanswered: How is the notion of self to be understood? In view of the failure of both introspection and scientific psychology to quell my appetite, I had then to look for another field within which to conduct my investigation. Because the initial question arose in relation to self as experienced in the everyday world, it seemed obvious that the arena in which to search would be the arena of the world of everyday life. Rather than theorize abstractly about how the notion of self might be understood, what seemed needed at that time was an analysis of the experienced self, understood within the context of the everyday world. Consequently, as a means of carrying out an investigation within the precincts of the everyday world, a framework of common sense was formulated—one based on the work of both George H. Mead[4] and Alfred Schutz.[5] Because of the emphasis placed upon the notion of experience, the cornerstone of the "reality" of the everyday world, the research was situated within the hermeneutical tradition. As a Ph.D. within the Faculty of Education at Monash University (Melbourne), this thesis showed me above all else that a concept such as "self" gains its meaning from within the terms of the conceptual framework within which it is being investigated. In other words, the notion of "self" cannot be said to have one definitive concep-tualization but, rather, will be conceptualized according to the particular-ity of the framework employed. This means that a question asked must be situated and explored within a specified frame of reference. What became most apparent to me was that failure to clarify and state the theoretical assumptions underpinning the framework utilized will inevitably lead to research difficulties. Unless we are clear as to the nature of the assump-tions that we make, we will not know what we still have on hand to work with in theory construction itself. The danger is, therefore, that unless taken-for-granteds are brought into relief and acknowledged, we run the risk of confusing theoretical presuppositions with theoretical formula-tions. Consequently, we can readily produce contradictory and illogical propositions.

My Question Within the Psychoanalytic Tradition

Not surprisingly, my search for self or personal truth led me to the domain of psychoanalysis. Here I faced the issue both in theory and practice. From the point of view of my own analysis, I personally experi-enced the disconcerting discovery of the unconscious and its effects. In addition, as a practitioner in the field of psychoanalysis I was challenged to conceptualize at a theoretical level what I dealt with in my day-to-day work. One crucial problem for me related to how psychoanalytic theory handled the issues of subject and agency. By this time I was better equipped to ask potentially productive questions than was previously the case. My question was now formulated as: How are the notions of subject and agency understood at a theoretical level within the psychoanalytic framework? For the purpose of the argument of this book the term *subject* refers specifically to the individual who speaks to the analyst, and the term *agency* to the notion of the determination or control of thoughts, words, and actions. Because in this book the subject refers to the subject who speaks to the analyst, we will necessarily deal with the theoretical conceptualization of the subject in the clinical situation.

My discovery of the unconscious, however, brought complications and complexities to this question. Such was the case because now I needed to contend with a situation in which the subject who speaks to the analyst does so in a very particular way—that is, both consciously and unconsciously—and, what is more, does this simultaneously. From the point of view of the speaker, the subject in the clinical situation, there is but one spoken discourse—that which is consciously intended. Nevertheless, psychoanalytic experience teaches us that the speaker unawaredly speaks another discourse, the discourse of the unconscious—one that is embedded within the conscious discourse and so available to the analyst's ear. If the speaker is unaware of this discourse, if it is not intended yet nevertheless has a meaning within the context of his or her life history, who then can be said to be the subject of such speech? Who is the agent of this conscious discourse, and who is the agent of the discourse of the unconscious? Are we to postulate the possibility of two subjects? If not, how are we to conceptualize this undeniably complex issue? How are we to understand the enigma of the double discourse? These were some of the many questions that gave impetus to the research presented in this book.

Before proceeding further it is important, I think, to make clear my own position in undertaking the work reported in the pages to follow. Although I no doubt have an affinity for some theoretical persuasions rather than others, especially in my own clinical work, the argument presented in *Which Is to Be Master?* is not based in any particular school of psychoanalytic thought. When I commenced this research, I attempted to distance myself and so view the psychoanalytic literature as a whole. It was in the process of reading the primary-source material from a "distanced stance" that the central problem became clear to me. My method is a straightforward logical analysis of the work of the great theorists in the field. In each instance I look for the essential components in any sound theory construction—namely, logical consistency and coherence.

Although my question has been rekindled within the domain of clinical psychoanalysis, I have chosen to give low salience to the experiential in the construction of my argument. My primary source material is comprised of the published works of Freud, Heinz Hartmann, Melanie Klein, and Jacques Lacan—all of whom use knowledge derived from the consulting room in their theory construction. Even though I do not myself draw on clinical examples, it will become clear to the reader that many problems regarding logical consistency arise out of the disjunction that is to be found between theory and practice. This is to be evidenced in the work of Freud and Lacan in particular.

I turned, then, first to Freud, the alpha of psychoanalysis; and in my own reading of the *Standard Edition*[6] I found that the question I brought to his work concerning the notions of subject and agency in psychoanalysis did not directly concern him in his theory construction. What I did discover, however, was that when confronted with a subject troubled with a problem of failed agency, Freud began to formulate his own unique conceptual system. Yet in so doing, his attempt to grapple at a theoretical level with the problems that he met in his clinical practice led him along a particular path. Rather than focus on the initial problem concerning subject and agency, Freud began to schematize the psychic apparatus. In his work he lost sight of the importance of the issues of subject and of agency and consequently ultimately proposed a topography of the mind unattached to any subject. Furthermore, embedded within his changing formulations are numerous logical inconsistencies and contradictions that relate to the assumptions made about the agency of the subject. In the main, Freud imputed agency to the apparatus. Thus he located the concept of agency apart or separated from the concept of the subject within the psychoanalytic framework of thought that he developed.

This separation of the concepts of subject and agency has had significant consequences for subsequent psychoanalytic theory construction. Those who adopt Freud's second topography in their own theories take with it a number of inherent problems of consistency as far as the concept of agency is concerned. In addition, if these theorists fail to question the nature of the link between subject and apparatus at a theoretical level, variations regarding the assumptions made about the subject in psychoanalysis are produced. This can be evidenced in the work of Heinz Hartmann and Melanie Klein. The former unwittingly works on the assumption of the sociological subject, whereas the latter assumes an innately moral subject.

One theorist, Jacques Lacan, has addressed the concepts directly. Yet Lacan, like Freud before him, conceptualizes subject and agency as separate variables. Lacan places emphasis upon the importance of language in his theory of the subject in psychoanalysis. For him the subject is structured, determined, or constituted by the symbolic order—that is, Lacan imputes agency to the symbolic order itself. This is a key theoretical postulate throughout his entire work, one that he never rescinds. Nevertheless, a reading of Lacan's published works throws into relief numerous instances where his assumptions about the subject in psychoanalysis are irreconcilable with his position concerning agency. Thus it is my argument that the separation of the concepts of subject and agency, found in psychoanalytic theory, is a core problem for theory construction.

In this book it is my aim, first, to trace in somewhat careful detail the way in which Freud's thought moved to produce what is so much associated with his work—namely, the second topography of the psychic apparatus. The chapters of the book that describe this initial analysis are lengthy. This I consider necessary because few theorists or writers who utilize the id, ego, and super-ego terminology ever attend to the nature of the assumptions that underlie their formulation. Because "the end is where we start from,"[7] it is important to explore the basis of that upon which we build if it is to be optimally productive. Second, it is my intention to provide an illustration of how the problem found in Freud's work can be seen to have influenced later psychoanalytic theorization. The work of Hartmann and Klein will be presented with an emphasis upon the assumptions made concerning the subject in psychoanalysis. Lacan's work will be presented with an emphasis upon the problem found in his separation of the concepts of agency and subject.

Finally, it is my aim to propose a solution to what I found to be a problem embedded within the core of psychoanalytic theory. This proposal involves the introduction of the concept of structuration to the field of psychoanalysis. The term *structuration* is derived from the work of the sociologist Anthony Giddens, but it takes on a meaning particular to the psychoanalytic domain. The advantage of this proposal is that it eliminates the need for the concept of agency and provides a new approach to the way in which the subject in psychoanalysis might be handled within theory construction.

Primary-Source Material

Before proceeding, it is necessary at the outset to point out that I have used primary-source material as far as is possible, particularly in the instances of Freud, Hartmann, and Klein. I have done so in the light of what I take to be the wisdom in the French saying *"Reculer pour sauter mieux."* However, because of the well-documented[8] difficulties inherent in Lacan's style as well as the slow publication of translated transcripts of his Seminars, I have found secondary-source material indispensable when dealing with his theory. I do not read any but school French. This is a limitation I accept and one that has, of course, placed restrictions on my access to unpublished primary-source material in Lacanian psychoanalytic theory. A consequence of this situation is that the Lacan presented here is the Lacan of the English-speaking world. To date, this is predominantly the early Lacan because only the published translations of a selection of his *Écrits*[9] as well as the transcripts of Seminars I,[10] II,[11] and XI[12] are available. Apart from a smattering of translated pieces published in psychoanalytic journals and edited collections, knowledge of the thought of the late Lacan can be gained through secondary-source material alone. In terms of the argument of this book, the problem identified in Lacan's early work is carried into his later theorization. This will be dealt with briefly through reference to commentaries on his work. It will be evident that greater access to Lacan's later Seminars would make no difference to my core argument.

A further related point about Lacan's work needs to be mentioned here: Lacan has written very few texts. His Seminars—the principal means of his transmission of psychoanalytic knowledge—were spoken and addressed, in the main, to psychoanalysts in training. Thus, even for French readers, these works have a special status. It could be said, therefore, that a logical analysis of such primary-source material as the Seminar transcripts is inappropriate because Lacan did not intend these texts for publication. Thus some might deem it unfair to criticize him for inconsistency given that his words were delivered in the Seminar situation where he was both creative and spontaneous.

It is my contention that since Lacan's Seminars and *Écrits* have been published, they, like any other written text, are available for analysis. Furthermore, it is really Lacan's thought itself, particularly the assumptions underpinning it, that will be the focus of our inquiry. This is so, irrespective of whether this is to be found in his articles for publication or published Seminar transcriptions. It is understood that the work of all great theorists involves a process of the transformation of their ideas and that what is proposed at one period may be inconsistent with a later or earlier formulation. The criterion of logical consistency applied within this work specifically refers to the underlying assumptions concerning the location of human agency within central tenets of a theorist's position at any given period.

Two issues with particular reference to Freud require brief discussion before turning to his work: the problem of translation and the level of theoretical explanation.

The Problem of Translation

Before proceeding to argue that Freud's theory lacked consistency and coherence, it is important to acknowledge a possible problem in terms of the accuracy of the translation used throughout this research.

Bruno Bettleheim, a psychoanalyst born into a middle-class assimilated Jewish family in Vienna fifty years later than Freud, has pointed out that much was the same in the Vienna he knew and the Vienna of Freud's time. He refers in particular to the spoken language. In *Freud and Man's Soul*[13] Bettleheim points to the need for correction of the translation of some of the most important psychoanalytic concepts. As this present research is based on J. Strachey's translation of *The Complete Works,* many of Bettleheim's alternative translations are of the utmost importance. The concept of the psyche, which is central to the present work, is translated by Bettleheim as "soul." He claims that "soul" is the best translation because of the many emotional connotations evoked by this word. According to Bettleheim, Freud often spoke of the soul—"of its nature and structure, its development, its attribute, how it reveals itself in all we do and dream."[14] Thus, where Strachey translates "mental apparatus" it would read better as "structure of the soul" and "mental organization," as "the organization of the soul." Bettleheim makes the point that if Freud had wanted an equivalent to "mental" he would have used the German word *geistig*. Although Freud never provides a precise definition of the term *soul*, Bettleheim writes:

> I suppose that he chose the term *because* of its inexactitude, its emotional resonance. Its ambiguity speaks for the ambiguity of the psyche itself, which reflects many different, warring levels of consciousness simultaneously. . . .
> I should point out however, that when Freud speaks of the soul he is talking about a psychological concept; it too is a metaphor. There is nothing supernatural about his idea of the soul . . . By "soul" or "psyche" Freud means that which is most valuable in man while he is alive . . . the soul is the seat both of the mind and of the passions. It is intangible, but it nevertheless exercises a powerful influence on our lives. It is what makes us human. . . .[15]

Some problems with translation can be accounted for in terms of the difference in linguistic properties and differences in underlying theoretical perspectives. As Bettleheim notes, the German language itself does justice to the ambiguities and contradictions that are composites of the unconscious, whereas English requires that such complexities be avoided. What is more, whereas many topics with which Freud dealt permit both a hermeneutic-spiritual and a positivistic-pragmatic approach, English translators generally opt for the latter because positivism is the most important English philosophical tradition. The result is, therefore, that Freud may well have been mistranslated and so misunderstood.

Nevertheless, what will be argued in this work is that, irrespective of this acknowledged possible problem of translation, Freud's inconsistency and incoherence is much more related to his failure to address questions concerning the assumptions made in his hypotheses than to a failure in the translation of his writings.

Levels of Explanation

Freud made numerous attempts to schematize the human psyche throughout his writings, which were in themselves a continual endeavor to conceptualize and so theorize upon the findings of his clinical experience. It is important to note that within Freud's causal explanation of

human behavior there are two levels of theorization that require differen-
tiation.

According to Ernst Mayr[16] there are two distinguishable causal approaches in the life sciences: the proximate-causal and the ultimate-causal.
The proximate-causal theorist is one who studies organic phenomena as
they manifest themselves in the individual's lifetime asking the question
"How come?" The ultimate-causal theorist studies organic phenomena
within the context of evolutionary biology asking the question "Why?"
The former theorist might ask questions such as "How come a person's
hormonal system can malfunction from eating a particular food?" whereas
the latter theorist might ask, within an evolutionary context, "Why do
human beings have a different hormonal system from those of other
species?" Freud was at times a proximate-causal theorist and at other
times an ultimate-causal theorist. Although his theory of the human mind
does involve both explanatory levels, this work is concerned with Freud
as proximate-causal theorist alone. This is so because the question asked
is best placed within a proximate-type explanatory framework, thereby
avoiding all biological complexities.

It is our work, now, to trace the origin and consequences of the
conceptual separation between the concepts of subject and agency in
psychoanalytic theory and to explore a possible alternative to the problem
posed.

THE PRESENTING PROBLEM

1

Subject and Agent: The Case of the *Hystérique d'Occasion*

It is a commonly held view that Freud's interest in hysteria and hypnosis gave birth to his psychoanalytic quest. This might be accounted for owing to the importance that Freud himself gave to hysteria and the cathartic method in both "On the History of the Psycho-Analytic Movement"[1] and *An Autobiographical Study.*[2] It is interesting to note that in both these texts he omitted any consideration of the crucial element in the early stages of his theorization: namely, the problem of a subject troubled with a failure in human agency. In my own reading of the *Standard Edition,* I found that it was precisely in the face of a woman who willed to breast-feed her baby but could not do so that Freud found impetus to commence his own theory construction. The instance referred to is the 1892–93 case of an *hystérique d'occasion.*

Not only was Freud initially challenged to understand the clinical presentation of failed agency, but as will be seen, his first classificatory system was also to be based on this very notion. Little attention has been given to this point. Rather, emphasis has been placed upon the sexual aspects of Freud's theory. In this chapter I will describe the movement in Freud's thought from the original conceptualization of a patient (subject) with a problem of willpower (agency) to the one of the concepts of ego and the repressed. It is in the light of his introduction of the pivotal notion of repression that many problems for theory construction ensue, particularly with regard to the concepts of subject and agency. The model that Freud developed via the movement in thought traced here will be referred to throughout this book as Freud's clinical model. In the chapters to follow, the development of what will be referred to as Freud's topographical model will be given consideration.

A Subject Affected with Weakened Agency

Freud's first actual case report, one that bears the mark of his earliest clinically based theory construction, was published contemporaneously with the better-known "Preliminary Communication" of 1893. His less-acknowledged paper is entitled "A Case of Successful Treatment by Hypnotism with Some Remarks on the Origin of Hysterical Symptoms Through 'Counter-Will' " and is found among the Pre-Psycho-Analytic Publications in the first volume of the *Standard Edition*.[3] In this paper Freud presents the case of a young woman between the ages of twenty to thirty years, whom he refers to in Jean Martin Charcot's phrase as an *"hystérique d'occasion."*[4] Freud reports that although "her capability, her quiet common sense and her naturalness made it impossible for anyone, including her family doctor, to regard her as a neurotic,"[5] she nevertheless exhibited debilitating symptoms arising from her efforts to feed her first child. This woman had a poor flow of milk, suffered pains when the baby was put to the breast, lost her appetite, and became sleepless; yet, when the baby was given to a wet nurse, her health returned. When, three years later, her second child was born, her attempts to feed the baby were even less successful, and more distressing symptoms became prominent. Freud was brought in to hypnotize the woman, and he reports that after two sessions she was cured by the use of the suggestion that contradicted all her fears and the feelings on which those fears were based:

> Have no fear! You will make an excellent nurse and the baby will thrive. Your stomach is perfectly quiet, your appetite is excellent, you are looking forward to your next meal, etc.[6]

However, given the "occasion" once more of bearing a child, the woman yet a second time called on Freud for assistance. From his point of view, he reports: "I found the patient in the same condition as the year before and positively exasperated with herself because her will could do nothing against her disinclination for food and her other symptoms . . ."[7] After the second hypnosis, the symptoms were so completely dealt with that a third session was not required. In the face of this successful treatment Freud notes: " 'I felt ashamed,' the woman said to me, 'that a thing like hypnosis should be successful where I myself, with all my willpower, was helpless.' "[8]

The First Nosology

It is clear from the foregoing case presentation that Freud's hypnotic treatment attempted to deal with the patient's struggle with what was experienced by her as a problem with agency—her willpower was, in this instance, ineffectual. No matter how much this woman may have wanted to eat, sleep, and breast-feed her baby successfully, she could not use her willpower to do so. This meant that the hypnotic suggestion was used as a means of contradicting or countering the symptoms. Here, symptoms were regarded by Freud as aspects of behavior that were outside the region of the control of conscious agency or willpower. It was from this vantage point that Freud conceptualized hysterical symptoms as "counter-will" when he began to consider what may have been the psychical mechanism of the woman's disorder. In essence Freud set out to understand the nature of the experience of a lack of willpower. His deductive solution to the problem that confronted him was as follows.

There are two types of ideas that have an expectancy attached to them. First, intentions—that is, ideas of my doing this or that—and, second, expectations—that is, ideas of this or that happening to me. The effect of expectancy attached to each is dependent on two factors: (1) the degree of importance of the outcome to the person; and (2) the degree of uncertainty inherent in the expectation of the outcome. According to Freud, "The subjective uncertainty, the counter-expectation, is itself represented by a collection of ideas to which I shall give the name of 'distressing antithetic ideas.' "[9] These are exemplified in the case of intention as thinking that one will not succeed because something is difficult or because of what might happen. In the case of an expectation, one thinks of all the things that could possibly happen other than the desired one. The healthy person deals with antithetic ideas with powerful self-confidence, suppressing and inhibiting these thoughts as far as is possible. The neurotic, however, having a tendency to depression and a lowered self-confidence, gives great attention to antithetic ideas against intentions.

This may be on account of the subject matter of the ideas fitting in with the mood of the neurosis or because antithetic ideas flourish in the soil of a neurosis.

When antithetic ideas relate to expectations, the result is a pessimistic frame of mind; if the antithetic ideas relate to intentions, *folie du doute* results. In terms of the different nervous states, Freud classified neurasthenia and hysteria quite separately according to the mechanism at work. In neurasthenia the pathologically intensified antithetic idea combines with the volitional idea. This combination forms a single act of consciousness. Because the antithetic idea takes away from the volitional idea, weakness of will is brought about in neurasthenia. In hysteria, the process differs in that the distressing antithetic idea is removed from association with the intention and continues to exist as a disconnected idea, often unconsciously in the patient. Another distinction is to be made between neurasthenia and hysteria. In hysteria, the inhibited antithetic idea can become realized by enervation of the body just as easily as does a volitional idea in normal circumstances. Freud explains: "The antithetic idea establishes itself, so to speak, as a 'counter-will,' while the patient is resolute but powerless."[10]

The above distinction can be seen from a clinical perspective. The case of this woman, prevented by neurotic difficulties from feeding her child, would have been evidenced quite differently if she had been a neurasthenic. Given the latter condition, she would have felt a conscious dread of the task before her, she would have been plagued by thoughts of possible accidents, and yet, given time she would have eventually fed the baby satisfactorily. If, alternatively, the antithetic idea had been more powerful, she probably would have abandoned the task altogether out of fear. Being a hysteric, this woman behaved differently. Although she may not have been conscious of her fear, she was determined to feed the child. Yet, she behaved "as though it was her will not to feed the child on any account."[11] Furthermore, this will evoked in her many symptoms to indispose her—loss of appetite, aversion to food, and pains when the child was put to her breast. It is this will, counter-will, that exercised greater control over her body than did conscious thought. Freud explains the difference in mechanisms in operation as follows:

> Here, in contrast to the *weakness* of will shown in neurasthenia, we have a *perversion* of will; and in contrast to the resigned resoluteness shown in the

former case, here we have astonishment and exasperation at a disunity which is incomprehensible to the patient.[12]

For Freud, at this point, hysterics were the helpless victims of their antithetic ideas when the emergence of a counter-will was responsible for the difficult characteristics or symptoms that they exhibited. The classificatory system developed and employed by Freud to distinguish between neurasthenia and hysteria was based on the fundamental concept of willpower. What instigated this development was the clinical problem of why a woman who so much wanted to feed her child was unable to do so.

Freud again mentions the concept of antithetic ideas in regard to the patient Frau Emmy Von N[13] and later describes the case in more detail in *Studies on Hysteria*.[14] Freud notes that Frau Von N suffered from the symptom of making a clacking noise with her tongue—this being, of course, against her will. He describes her as "a hysterical lady who showed great strength of will in those of her dealings which were unaffected by her illness; but in those which *were* so affected she showed no less clearly the weight of the burden imposed on her by her numerous and oppressive hysterical impediments and incapacities."[15] Frau Von N, therefore, suffered from a perversion of will. Similarly, in the famous case of Anna O, Josef Breuer, Freud's teacher and friend, talks of two states of consciousness persisting side by side: one in which willpower is normal; the other in which it is incapacitated.[16] Breuer's "hypnoid states" might well be identified with that state in which counter-will asserts itself.

Following this formulation of the first nosology Freud shifted his interest toward the idea of defense, then finally toward the concept of repression. In each movement we will see a gradually waning interest in the commonsense idea of human agency through willpower and a growing interest in what eventually became defined as the unconscious process of repression, an agency about which the subject has no conscious knowledge.

Will and Defense

From a theoretical point of view Breuer and Freud had come to a number of conclusions concerning the phenomenon of hysteria which they published in their 1893–95 *Studies on Hysteria*.[17] Breuer held that hysteria, specifically hypnoid hysteria, is caused by a splitting of consciousness in the sense that something traumatic happens to a person that s/he cannot remember but that it happens while the person is in a particular state of mind akin to that which is experienced in hypnosis. The associated ideas find no resistance while the person is in this hypnoid state. Freud initially accepted Breuer's postulation but later refused to hold to it as explained in his 1896 paper "The Aetiology of Hysteria."[18]

In *Studies on Hysteria* both he and Breuer agreed upon what they termed retention hysteria. This type of hysteria finds its origin in a past traumatic situation, one that the patient was unable to deal with from a psychological point of view at the time when it took place. The experience is not cathected—that is, the excitation caused is denied an outlet, such as telling someone else what happened—and so sometimes becomes converted into a somatic expression. Breuer thought that hypnoid hysteria was the more common but noted Freud's suggestion of yet a third type of hysteria that was to take the latter along a particularly fruitful path—namely, defense hysteria:

> Freud has found in the deliberate amnesia of defense a second source, independent of hypnoid states, for the construction of ideational complexes which are excluded from associative contact.[19]

Earlier in the same paper Breuer defined defenses as "the deliberate suppression of distressing ideas which seem to the subject to threaten his happiness or his self-esteem."[20] Furthermore, mentioning Freud's paper "The Neuro-Psychoses of Defense"[21] in which he discusses the process of defense, Breuer adds: "We cannot, it is true, understand how an idea can be deliberately repressed from consciousness."[22] Clearly, defense presented a problem to Breuer, but it was Freud who pressed his theorization in that direction rather than toward hypnoid or retention hysteria: "It is to be hoped that fresh observation will soon decide whether I am running the risk of falling into one-sidedness and error in thus favoring an extension of the concept of defense to the whole of hysteria."[23]

Will and Repression

At this time, Freud used the concept of defense interchangeably with the concept of repression. In some of its earliest appearances the term *repressed (verdrängt)* is accompanied by the adverb *intentionally (absichtlich)* or by *deliberately (willkürlich)*, as for example, in the 1893 "Preliminary Communication" where retention hysteria is described as follows:

> In the first group are those cases in which the patients have not reacted to a psychical trauma because the nature of the trauma excluded a reaction, as in the case of the apparently irreparable loss of a loved person or because social circumstances made a reaction impossible or because it was a question of things which the patient wished to forget, and therefore intentionally repressed from his conscious thought and inhibited and suppressed.[24]

In "The Psychotherapy of Hysteria"[25] Freud explains that, by means of his clinical work, he had overcome a psychical force in the patients that was opposed to the pathogenic ideas becoming conscious—that is, remembered. It was, he argued, that same force that played a part in both generating the hysterical symptom and in preventing the pathogenic idea from becoming conscious. Furthermore, Freud held that this clinical resistance, to be theoretically understood as the concept of repression, was an endeavor to keep distressing ideas out of consciousness. These ideas "were all of a kind that one would prefer not to have experienced, that one would rather forget."[26] The notion of censoring distressing ideas or defending against ideas incompatible to the individual's consciousness was understood to be the work of the ego:

> Thus a psychical force, aversion on the part of the ego, had originally driven the pathogenic idea out of association and was now opposing its return to memory. The hysterical patient's "not knowing" was in fact a "not wanting to know"—a not wanting which might be to a greater or less extent conscious.[27]

We are left with the important question, then, of to what extent the patient's will was thought to be involved in the process of repression, of defense. According to Strachey the word *intentionally* simply indicates the existence of a motive but carries no implication of conscious intention.[28] This argument does not seem in line with the whole thrust of the 1896 paper on which Strachey draws to provide evidence in reference to the concept of repression or defense. It would seem far more accurate to argue that the question of whether will was or was not involved in the act of defense was a specific problem for Freud at this stage particularly in the light of his attention to the problem of willpower in the hysterical patient as described earlier. In his 1896 paper where he is much more explicit about the notion of defense in the neuropsychoses, which by then included phobias and obsessions, Freud discusses the process of defense, contrary to Strachey's note, employing the important concept of will.

Freud argues that it is impossible to regard the splitting of consciousness in two forms of hysteria as primary in Pierre Janet's sense. Janet was a French follower of Charcot who was interested in states of dissociation. Freud states that:

> I was repeatedly able to show that *the splitting of the content of consciousness is the result of an act of will on the part of the patient;* that is to say, it is initiated by an effort of will whose motive can be specified. By this I do not, of course, mean that the patient intends to bring about a splitting of his consciousness. His intention is a different one; but instead of attaining its aim, it produces a splitting of consciousness.[29]

In other words, defense is the intentional act of the will, not the splitting of consciousness.

That Freud held defense to be a conscious intention is even more clearly stated in the same paper where he explains the role of will in the patient's memory of what happened at the time of the origin of the symptom:

> Furthermore, the most unambiguous statements by the patients give proof of the effort of will, the attempt at defense, upon which the theory lays emphasis, and at least in a number of cases the patients themselves inform us that their phobia or obsession made its first appearance after the effort of will had apparently succeeded in its aim. "Something very disagreeable happened to me once and I tried very hard to put it away from me and not to think about it any more. I succeeded at last; but then I got this other thing, which I have not been able to get rid of since."[30]

It seems, therefore, that at this stage of his theorization Freud did think defense was brought about by the conscious will of the patient, but his constant use of the concept of the ego introduced a problem to this understanding of the process of defense.

Freud talked of the role of the ego in defending incompatible ideas in his 1894 paper in much the same vein as in "The Psychotherapy of Hysteria" but with a clear indication that he took defense to be a conscious and purposeful act. The ego, he said, was faced with an incompatible experience, idea, or feeling and that "the subject decided to forget it because he had no confidence in his power to resolve the contradiction between that incompatible idea and his ego by means of thought—

activity."[31] It is important to note here that defense, understood as an act of the will, raises a theoretical problem in reference to the relationship between the subject, the ego, and willpower. One is introduced very early to a crucial problem that consistently blights Freudian theory: namely, the confusion surrounding Freud's theoretical presuppositions regarding the nature of human agency. It is difficult to ascertain what attributes Freud assumes pertain to each of his concepts. For example, who wills defense? Is it the ego, the subject, or is the ego synonymous with the subject? In the instance above the subject would seem to be the one who wills and who employs his ego in the service of defense, whereas in a previously quoted description of the ego (p. 19) the latter seems to be the agent itself. The difference in conceptualizations of the ego is most apparent where Feud writes of either the ego, assuming agency on the part of the ego, or the individual's or subject's ego, assuming agency on the part of the subject. Much attention will be given to this problem throughout the work to follow.

The Changed Nosology

By 1898 Freud had moved from his initial classificatory system of nervous disorders. Whereas he had thought in terms of neurasthenia and hysteria, differing on the basis of the mechanism utilized with regard to willpower, he next thought in terms of a classificatory system that employed the concepts, the actual neuroses, and the psychoneuroses. The new classificatory system was understood, not in terms of the mechanism utilized with regard to willpower, but on the basis of the sexual etiology of the problems experienced. The actual neuroses were distinguished by virtue of their connection with sexual problems of the present: neurasthenia was held to be caused by immoderate masturbation or spontaneous emissions; whereas anxiety neuroses were caused by enforced abstinence, unconsummated genital excitement, or coition that was imperfect or interrupted. The psychoneuroses, however, were understood in terms of *past* sexual experiences and in terms of differing mechanisms of defense employed in each category. Indeed, by 1896 in "Further Remarks on the Neuro-Psychoses of Defense"[32] Freud could say quite definitively that hysteria, obsessions, and certain cases of hallucinatory confusion, grouped together as the neuropsychoses of defense, had one aspect in common: "This was

that their symptoms arose through the psychical mechanism of (unconscious) *defense*—that is, in an attempt to repress an incompatible idea
which had come into distressing opposition to the patient's ego."[33] This
change in his understanding of the process of defense was extremely
significant. This is so because once defense was no longer simply an act of
the will, conceptualization of the process at an unconscious level allowed
Freud to enrich, through elaboration, his theory of neuroses. As already
noted, prior to 1896 Freud held that hysteria could be traced to a psychical conflict arising through an incompatible idea setting in action a defense on the part of the ego and calling upon a demand for continued
repression. At this stage he did not hold that defense or repression in
itself was pathological but that sometimes it resulted in pathological
symptoms. On the basis of his now "sexual" rather than "willpower"
orientation Freud was able to provide more information regarding when
pathological effects were brought into being in his 1896 paper "The
Aetiology of Neuroses":

> *The defense achieves its purpose of thinking the incompatible idea out of conscious-
> ness if there are infantile sexual scenes present in the (hitherto normal) subject in
> the form of unconscious memories, and if the idea that is to be repressed can be
> brought into logical or associative connection with an infantile experience of that
> kind.*[34]

Here, Freud gives potency to "the defense" rather than to the subject
who, in this instance, undergoes the process passively. Furthermore, the
importance of memory is highlighted within Freud's changing understanding of the psychology of neuroses. Unconscious memory can be
associatively linked with an idea and so brings pathological effect into
being. Why it was only ideas of a sexual nature that caused pathological
repression became a key question for Freud. He had, however, addressed
the problem of why childhood traumas operate in a deferred fashion. This
latter notion led to the fruitful paper "Screen Memories,"[35] which discusses the unconscious mechanism of displacement at work in those
memories that are not as important for their own content as they are to
the content of memories that are related to the screen memory but have
been repressed.

By the late 1890s, Freud had years of clinical experience behind him.
In light of his work with neurotic patients during these years, he had
formulated a clinical model that informed his day-to-day practice. This
model is one in which the ego is imputed with agency. Although the ego

is generally efficacious against unacceptable, sexually related thought activity, symptoms form when there is a failure in the ego's ability to repress the incompatible idea.

Conclusion

By the turn of the century Freud had moved a distance from his point of departure when confronted with the *hystérique d'occasion*. This movement was from a nosology based on aberrations of willpower to one based on unconscious memories and mechanisms of defense. This means that his understanding of mental illness had undergone a radical change. With this change came the introduction of key concepts such as the ego, repression, and the unconscious, within a developing psychological theory of the human subject that no longer investigated man's psychical life within the terms of a commonsense approach. Because Freud's theorization moved to the realm of the unconscious, he required a means of conceptualizing the subject that had never been attempted before. Freud's theory needed to incorporate the notion of counter-will understood in terms of symptom, defense understood in terms of repression, and the will understood in terms of the ego. This shift was not a simple movement indicative of a one-to-one correspondence of terms but a fundamentally different construction of the subject.

One of Freud's main problems in building a theory can be attributed to his failure to specify and clarify the nature of the theoretical assumptions that he made in regard to the problem of the subject in psychoanalysis. In particular, he was never clear as to where he located the notion of agency and consequently continually took it for granted that this capacity lay wherever his theory required it to be for the point of discussion at the time. His failure to specify this crucial element underpinning his theory meant that he was never in the position to know what was left to be conceptualized and thus to be employed in the theory itself. This is not to say that Freud needed to philosophize regarding the nature of the subject in psychoanalysis because that would, in all probability, lead to the arena of metaphysics and toward a field that he adamantly refrained from entering: "We have nothing to expect from philosophy except that it will once again haughtily point out to us the intellectual inferiority of the object of our study."[36] It is to say, however, that problems of conceptualization and theorization resulted from his failure to state his pretheoretical assumptions. Freud's movement away from an interest in willpower resulted in his leaving aside the question of human agency from this point onward in his theoretical postulations. The focus of his theory building became, instead, the psychical apparatus.

In the following four chapters we will investigate Freud's attempts to schematize what he terms the psychic apparatus. Freud's emphasis upon conceptualizing the psyche in schematic form will be shown to lead him to neglect at a theoretical level that which underpinned his work: namely, the nature of his assumptions concerning the subject and agency in psychoanalysis.

FREUD'S SCHEMAS OF
THE MIND

2

The Freud-Fliess Correspondence: The First and Second Schemas

The Letters

Wilhelm Fliess (1858–1928), a Berlin nose-and-throat specialist, was advised by Josef Breuer to attend some of the lectures on the anatomy and mode of functioning of the nervous system that Freud was then giving at the University of Vienna. A mutual attraction arose between the two men in the scientific discussions that followed, and so began a correspondence that lasted from 1887 to 1904.

When the friendship ended, Freud either lost or destroyed the letters that Fliess had written to him. The Freud-Fliess correspondence, however, was preserved; and following Fliess's death in 1928, his widow sold the packet of 284 letters plus manuscripts and scientific notes to Reinhold Stahl, a Berlin bookseller, on the condition that they were not to be sold to Freud himself. When Stahl fled to France during the Nazi regime, he offered the documents to Mme. Marie Bonaparte, one of Freud's favorite pupils and analysands, who immediately bought them. Bonaparte told Freud, who offered to pay half the cost, but she refused realizing that Freud might then have rights over them as he wanted to. The correspondence journeyed to final safety via the Rothschild Bank in Vienna, the Danish Legation in Paris, and across the English Channel to London.

In 1950 a selection of these letters became public in a German edition of the correspondence, and in 1954 an English translation of this was published by Imago entitled *The Origins of Psycho-Analysis: Letters to*

Wilhelm Fliess, Drafts and Notes, 1887–1902, by Sigmund Freud. These publications were edited by Marie Bonaparte (Paris), Anna Freud (London), and Ernst Kris (New York). In both editions only 168 of the 284 letters available to the editors were published. The reason given in the editors' note reads as follows:

> The selection was made on the principle of making public everything relating to the writer's scientific work and scientific interests and everything bearing on the social and political conditions in which psycho-analysis originated and of omitting or abbreviating everything publication of which would be inconsistent with professional or personal confidence.[1]

In 1979 Jeffrey Mousaieff Masson approached Anna Freud to seek access to all documents from 1887 onward. With K. R. Eissler's support[2] Anna Freud gave Masson the necessary authority and, including documents located at the Jewish National and University Library in Jerusalem, at Maresfield Gardens, Hampstead, and in Robert Fliess's private collection, all are presented in Masson's new edition of 1985. There are 133 letters[3] presented for the first time as well as publication with no deletions of those already available in the 1954 edition. The Masson translation is used in the present work. The choice of this translation in preference to the 1954 *Origins* has been made to ensure that, given any anti-Freud tenor that might be found in the translation of the correspondence, it does not alter an argument built on theoretical rather than personal grounds.[4] However, the Strachey translation of the "Project" is used because, to quote Masson:

> And the 1895 "Project for a Scientific Psychology," Freud's construction of a theory of the mind, has been omitted because it would be difficult to improve on James Strachey's translation, published and still available in his *Standard Edition of the Complete Works of Sigmund Freud.*[5]

The First Schema: "Project for a Scientific Psychology"

One of the less-known yet nonetheless important manuscripts found among Freud's prepsychoanalytic publications is his "Project for a Scientific Psychology." This text was never published by Freud; as already indicated, it appeared in London in its first published version, in German, in 1950. Regardless of the evidence that Freud had wanted the manuscript to be disregarded, his letters to Fliess before and after writing it in late 1895 clearly indicate how central it was to his thinking during this period. Although the problems of the etiology of the neuroses and of defense absorbed Freud's thoughts in the 1895–96 period, he was nevertheless drawn to theorize about the psychical apparatus. This interest continued throughout fifty or so productive years. Freud knew that without some clarity of formulation in this area his clinical application could well flounder for want of a firm theoretical base. The importance to Freud of an attempt to theorize about the human psyche can be gleaned from the correspondence.

In a letter of April 27, 1895, Freud writes: "Scientifically, I am in a bad way; namely, caught up in "The Psychology for Neurologists," which regularly consumes me totally until, actually overworked, I must break off. I have never before experienced such a high degree of preoccupation. And will anything come of it? I hope so, but it is difficult and slow going."[6] The full fervor of his endeavor is best evidenced in his letter of May 25, 1895. He reports to Fliess that he has had an "inhuman amount to do," thus he has failed to correspond as he would have wished, but further:

> The main reason, however, was this: a man like me cannot live without a hobbyhorse, without a consuming passion, without—in Schiller's word— a tyrant. I have found one. In its service I know no limits. It is psychology, which has always been my distant, beckoning goal, and which now, since I have come upon the problem of neuroses, has drawn so much nearer. I am tormented by two aims; to examine what shape the theory of mental functioning takes if one introduces quantitative considerations, a sort of economics of nerve forces; and, second, to peel off from psychopathology a gain for normal psychology. Actually, a satisfactory general conception of neuropsychotic disturbances is impossible if one cannot link it with clear assumptions about normal mental processes. During the past week I have devoted every free minute to such work; have spent the hours of the night from eleven to two with such fantasizing, interpreting and guessing, and invariably stopped only when somewhere I came up against an absurdity or when I actually seriously overworked, so that I had no interest left in my daily medical activities. It will still be a long time before you can ask me about results.[7]

This all-consuming psychology for neurologists was mentioned in a sequence of Freud's letters to Fliess: June 12, August 6, October 8, October 15, October 20, November 29, and January 1, 1896. These letters reveal the intellectual difficulties that Freud faced in his attempt to cope with his "tyrant." It was with his October 8, 1895, correspondence that Freud enclosed two notebooks for Fliess's appraisal. There was, however, an acknowledged omission—a notebook dealing with the concept of repression at a theoretical level. The importance for Freud of the interchange between theory and practice is clearly enunciated in this letter:

> Now, the two notebooks. I scribbled them full at one stretch since my return, and they will bring little that is new to you. I am retaining a third notebook that deals with the psychopathology of repression, because it pursues its topic only to a certain point. From there on I had to work once again with new drafts and in the process became alternately proud and overjoyed and ashamed and miserable—until now, after an excess of mental torment, I apathetically tell myself. It does not yet, perhaps never will, hang together. What does not yet hang together is not the mechanism—I can be patient about that—but the elucidator of repression, the clinical knowledge of which has in other respects greatly progressed.[8]

In his letter of November 8, 1895, Freud again mentions his "tyrant": "I rebelled against my tyrant. I felt overworked, irritated, confused and incapable of mastering it all. So I threw everything away."[9] Yet, he resumed work on it and on January 1, 1896, sent Fliess a revision of his earlier proposals: "Your remarks on migraine have led me to an idea, as a consequence of which all my (present) theories would need to be completely revised—something I cannot venture to do now. I shall try to give you some idea of it, however."[10]

Freud's "Project"

We turn now to the "Project," considered here as Freud's first attempted schema of the human psyche. Freud's "Project for a Scientific Psychology," which he commenced putting on paper while still in the railroad car following a visit to see Fliess in Berlin, is composed of three main parts: (1) General Scheme; (2) Psychopathology; and (3) Attempt to Present Normal ψ Processes. This model is a neurological one based on two fundamental hypotheses: (1) the hypothesis of the neurone, which is the basis of the topographical or structural point of view that will be the focus of attention throughout the present work; and (2) the hypothesis of quantity, the basis of the economic point of view that will be described in chapter 4 with reference to Freud's metapsychology. Although the text contains five diagrams, none of these depicts the topographical layout that he presents in the description of the General Scheme. This scheme must be placed within the context of a much larger intellectual endeavor—a full psychology. It is, however, basic to the "Project" itself. To assist in an explanation of this scheme for present purposes, a version of R. Wollheim's[11] diagram will be used. This figure depicts three different neurological systems which are designated by Freud as ϕ (phi), ψ (psi) and ω (omega). These systems comprise the organism's psychical apparatus, providing the individual with the functional ability to register experience and remember it and to tolerate an accumulation of energy, which Freud denotes with Q (quantity).

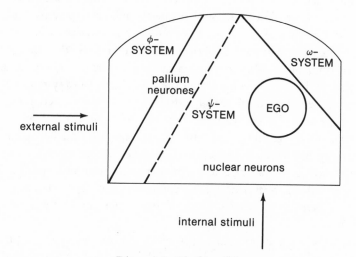

Diagram 1: The First Schema

The systems, although linked, are differentiated by the nature of the neurones involved. ψ is a system of permeable neurones that filter out and reduce stimulation. These neurones have a cutaneous barrier that provides protection from external stimuli. ω is a system of neurones that is to some degree impermeable and offers some resistance to the flow of energy. The latter is governed by the primary processes and essentially corresponds to the unconscious in later conceptualizations. This system provides for memory. ω is a system of neurones that gives qualities—that is, the experience of consciousness or perception—but that never receives quantity. This system falls alongside the ψ system. Freud accounted for the ability of the mental to store energy by postulating the notion of contact-barriers, those permanently "cathected" neurones in the ψ system.

The mind receives two types of stimuli, external and internal—the external stimuli being received by the ϕ system, the internal by the ψ system. The latter system is subdivided into nuclear neurones and pallium neurones—the distinction is not important here other than in passing to mention the direction of energy flow; quantity originating from an internal source flows outward through the nuclear neurones through the pallium toward the ϕ system and so ultimately toward the motor part of the apparatus. What brings this flow into action is referred to as a wishful state—in other words, the mind can operate under the influence of a wish. The wish seeks satisfaction either from the outer world of reality and/or the inner world of fantasy. Because the mental apparatus tends to operate so that pleasure is secured and unpleasure avoided, a number of processes are needed in the face of the wish: reality testing, defense against pain, thinking, judging, and remembering, and so forth. Freud postulated the notion of the ego, a group of neurones that lie in the ψ system, which had a directive or active role assigned to it. In this schema there could be too much reality for consciousness to handle because there are both perceptual reality, coming from the external barrier, and hallucinatory reality, resulting from internal stimulation. The role of the ego, which is the nucleus of the ψ system, is to permit external reality alone to function so that, in effect, its function is essentially inhibitive. It endeavors to prevent hallucination—it tries to cut off the excess coming from internal excitation.

There is a core, or nucleus, ego and some mobile portion that is constituted by processes on which the inhibiting influence is exercised. It is the latter secondary processes that will in later conceptualizations be represented by the preconscious-conscious system. As well as accounting for "specific actions," preestablished instinctual actions to achieve relief from hunger, endogenous stimuli (later to become instincts), respiration, and sex that are in conformity with reality, the ego is able to use energy at its disposal so that unpleasure is not experienced. This inhibition of unpleasure Freud referred to as primary defense. There is no need to go into the fine details of Freud's exposition here, but we can already see that he postulated a neurologically based psychology of the mind that included not only the simple reflex arc of stimulus (acquisition of energy)-response (giving off energy) but also the more complex possibility of internal stimuli, the notion of wish and the idea of hallucinatory satisfaction of a wish. What is important, nevertheless, is to understand that Freud did attempt to draw up a neurological account of the mind that aimed at corresponding to the anatomy known at the time:

> The hypothesis of there being two systems of neurones, ϕ and ψ, of which ϕ consists of permeable elements and ψ of impermeable seems to provide an explanation of this one of the peculiarities of the nervous system—that of retaining and yet of remaining capable of receiving . . .
>
> It will be objected against our hypothesis of contact—barriers that it assumes two classes with a fundamental difference in their conditions of functioning though there is at the moment no other basis for the differentiation. At all events, morphologically (that is, histologically) nothing is known in support of the distinction . . .
>
> Where else are we to look for this division into classes? If possible in the biological development of the nervous system . . .[12]

Because Freud was working within a neurological framework, he talked of all processes conceptualized within the terms of that particular domain. For example, he defined the ego whose work has been described as follows:

> Thus the ego is to be defined as the totality of the ψ cathexes, at the given time in which a permanent component is distinguished from a changing one.[13]

With regard to the function or organizing capacity of the ego in relation to the wish, he wrote:

> We have brought forward the hypothesis that, during the process of wishing, inhibition by the ego brings about a moderated cathexis of the object wished for, which allows it to be cognized as not real . . .[14]

Or again, the ego in relation to the process of judging is described as:

> Thus *judging* is a ψ process which is only made possible by inhibition by the ego and which is evoked by the dissimilarity between *wishful cathexes* of a memory and a perceptual cathexes that is similar to it.[15]

In both these processes, wishing and judging, defined neurologically, there is no mention of an active subject. Freud talks in terms of "the organism" and the processes that take place within the confines of the neurological apparatus. Who judges? Who wishes? The ego, the individual, or the cognizer? Freud is not at all clear. The wish itself is defined in neurological terms so that there is no recognition of a unique and will-full subject:

> The wishful state results in a positive *attraction* towards the object wished-for, or more precisely towards its mnemic image; the experience of pain leads to a repulsion, a disinclination to keeping the hostile mnemic image cathected.[16]

As indicated in chapter 1, Freud had been very interested in the problem of willpower and used the concept in his later work *The Psycho-pathology of Everyday Life*.[17] In the "Project" he defines it as follows:

> Here ψ is at the mercy of Q, and it is thus that in the interior of the system there arises the impulsion which sustains all psychical activity. We know this power as the *will*—the derivative of the *instincts*.[18]

What the connection is between the subject and will is never attended to, so that we are left with concepts such as wish, will, and ego that all contribute to the working of the organism. One further comment is needed here in reference to the role of the ego: that concerning patholog-ical defense.

In the "Project" Freud relates pathological defense to the organism's memory in such a way that he requires the notion of deferred action. This concept will be given brief consideration in the section to follow. In the meantime Freud linked the ego with this defense just as he was doing in his clinical practice—that is, as the agent of defense:

> By that means the release of unpleasure was quantitatively restricted, and its start was precisely a signal for the ego to set normal defense in action . . . Thus it is the ego's business not to permit any release of affect, because this at the same time permits a primary process. . . . in the case of the hysterical (compulsion). . . . Here . . . is no perception but a memory, which unex-pectedly releases unpleasure, and the ego only discovers this too late. It has permitted a primary process because it did not expect one.[19]

Even though Freud had not worked out his paper on repression, as already mentioned, it is clear at this early stage of his theorization that the whole area of defense was vitally important to his work.

In the introduction to the "Project" Strachey points out that it can be suggested that the human nervous system be regarded as similar to or even identical with an electronic computer—both of them machines for the reception, storage, processing, and output of information: "It has been plausibly pointed out that in the complexities of the 'neuronal' events described here by Freud, and the principles governing them, we may see more than a hint or two at the hypotheses of information theory and cybernetics in their application to the nervous system."[20] Freud's neurological model does indeed strike one as a computer information-processing model, one devoid of the notion of the human subject. Yet, this model must be understood within the context of Freud's life work. Within the terms of this understanding the importance of the "Project" is best viewed retrospectively—several of its postulations can be seen in a new form in Freud's later writings.[21]

Although Freud wrote to Fliess in his January 1, 1896, letter about changing his topographical placements of the neurones so that the ω neurones were now to be understood between the ϕ and the ψ neurones, it was not long before he attempted a new type of conceptualization of the mental apparatus, as will be discussed in the section to follow. Be that as it may, and given that, as Strachey points out, Freud did eventually "throw over the whole neurological framework,"[22] it is important for present purposes to see that Freud neglected here, as elsewhere, to specify the assumptions that he made regarding the nature of the subject in psychoanalysis. One has to remember that Freud was writing to Fliess. Therefore the nature of his conceptualizations bore the mark of that particular association. At this time Fliess was Freud's only reader—a reader with a similar background to Freud's. Both men were doctors and their common language was that of neurology, physiology, and anatomy. Their shared assumptions about the material of their correspondence, although remaining unarticulated, were clearly those of the scientific enterprise. These assumptions were never questioned, but simply taken for granted. As a consequence Freud produced a type of neurological computer model of mental processes that, from a theoretical point of view, did not require the underpinning notion of subject. People could be assumed to be machines or biological organisms waiting for that stimulus, either external or internal, which would set the reflex process in motion. This is so even if the translation tends toward a mechanistic account rather than Bettleheim's "soul-filled" account of Freud's writings. The definitions of wish and will provide clear evidence of the lack of an assumed human subject who has at times to come to terms with will versus counter-will in day-to-day life—that is, a subject who wills and wishes, not a neurophysiological apparatus. Furthermore, the problem of agency for Freud is exemplified in this model via the concept of the ego already described. At times Freud writes of the ego as a neurological agency, yet at others the ego is portrayed as that which is acted upon. J. Laplanche has captured this problem concerning the ego so precisely that his argument will be reported at length:

> The *Project for a Scientific Psychology* of 1895 posits the ego at the outset as not being essentially a *subject:* it is neither the subject in the sense of classical philosophy, a subject of perception and consciousness (it is not ω), nor the subject of wishing and desire, that subject which addresses us psychoanalysts: it is not the whole of ψ, nor even the essential part of ψ, but a specific formation within the mnemic systems, an internal object cathected by the energy of the apparatus. That *object* however, is capable of action, and it enters into conflicts as a participant by virtue of its double function: an inhibiting function or a function of binding . . . and a defensive function . . . through the dual modes of pathological and normal defence. Thus no sooner have we presented the thesis that the ego is not a subject than we have to withdraw it: the ego is indeed an object, but a kind of relay object, capable of passing itself off, in a more or less deceptive and usurpatory manner, as a desiring and wishing subject.[23]

Not only does this paragraph state the problem well, but it also states it in terms of the ambiguities and difficulties that Bettleheim has suggested are part of the German language.

The problem of agency is central even within the neurological context. That Freud did not forward the section on Repression, the third book, is interesting especially in the light of the argument of the previous chapter that he was perplexed as to how and why repression took place. If it was not the product of willpower, then why repression? Who represses? On what basis? Once repression is introduced, the concept of the unconscious is necessary and Freud's failure to handle repression at this stage meant a failure to incorporate the idea of the unconscious within the schema of the "Project." His clinical experience was beyond his theoretical acumen at this point. Furthermore, the concept of repression raises problems for the notion of the subject in psychoanalysis and how one might adequately conceptualize the possibility of a subject who wills but does not will—in other words, who is split. Freud's failure to address the problem adequately means that he was able to bypass some of the most vexing problems of his psychoanalytic endeavor. However, like the return of the repressed, it is these very same problems that were later to beset him time and time again whether he recognized them or not. It is an argument of this book that it was not until Lacan reconsidered the work of Freud, rereading it in a new light, that the problem of the subject of psychoanalysis was taken into account on a theoretical level.

The Second Schema: Speculation Anew

In the Freud-Fliess correspondence of January 1, 1896, Freud has not only rethought his ϕ ψ ω but also included in his correspondence Draft K, titled "The Neuroses of Defense (A Christmas Fairy Tale)." Central to this Draft is the concept of repression and its place in the varying neuroses:

> The main difference between the various neuroses are shown in the way in which the repressed ideas return; others are seen in the manner in which the symptoms are formed and in the course taken by the illness. But the specific character of a particular neurosis lies in the fashion in which the repression is accomplished.[24]

Alongside domestic news Freud continues to report to Fliess his growing conviction about the place of sexuality and repression in the etiology of the psychoneuroses, refining his ideas to the point where he can write on May 30, 1896:

> Surplus of sexuality alone is not enough to cause repression; the cooperation of *defense* is necessary, but without a surplus of sexuality defense does not produce a neurosis. . . .
> Thus the periods at which repression occurs are of no significance for the choice of neurosis; the periods at which the event occurs are decisive. The nature of the scene is of importance insofar as it is able to give rise to defense.[25]

By December 6, 1896, Freud is ready to speculate anew. This time his interest is less ambitious than his earlier attempt to provide a psychology for neurologists—this time he presents Fliess with a schema of the psychical apparatus, one that deals with the concept of memory traces as well as the concept of repression. We must remember that this speculation is included within a letter to Fliess—thus it is communicated in its barest outline. Freud proposed that the psychic mechanism comes into being by a process of stratification and that material in the form of memory traces is subjected from time to time to a rearrangement in accordance with fresh circumstances—to what he refers to as a retranscription. The core of his presentation and what is essentially new about this theory is the thesis "that memory is present not once but several times over, that it is laid down in various kinds of indications."[26] He links this notion with earlier work that he had done on aphasia and does so throughout his later work. Freud suggests three registrations, emphasizing that different registrations are separated (not necessarily topographically) according to the neurones that are their vehicles.

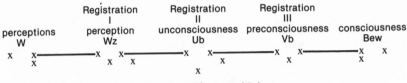

Diagram 2: The Second Schema

This schema is explained by Freud as follows:

> W (*Wahrnehmungen* [perceptions]) are neurones in which *perceptions* originate, to which consciousness attaches, but which in themselves retain no trace of what has happened. For *consciousness and memory are mutually exclusive*.
>
> Wz (*Wahrnehmungszeichen* [indication of perception]) is the first registration of the perceptions; it is quite incapable of consciousness and is arranged according to associations by simultaneity.
>
> Ub (Unbewusstsein [unconsciousness]) is the second registration, arranged according to other, perhaps causal, relations. Ub traces would perhaps correspond to conceptual memories; equally inaccessible to consciousness.
>
> Vb (*Vorbewusstsein* [preconsciousness]) is the third transcription, attached to word presentation and corresponding to our official ego. The cathexes proceeding from this Vb become conscious according to certain rules; and this secondary *thought consciousness* is subsequent in time and is probably linked to the hallucinatory activation of word presentations, so that the neurones of consciousness would once again be perceptual neurones and in themselves without memory.[27]

Although it is not specified by Freud, *Bew* represents *Bewusstsein* (consciousness).

As in the "Project" there is a flow of energy, and the schema is neurologically based. Each successive registration represents the psychic achievement of successive epochs of life. Here we can see an intermesh of two levels of theorization, proximate and ultimate. Freud proposed that at the boundary between two epochs a translation of the psychic material must take place and that the psychoneuroses are explained in terms of repression—that is, when normal translation has not taken place. Normal defense, which makes itself felt owing to a generation of unpleasure, occurs within one and the same psychic phrase and among registrations of the same kind. In contrast, pathological defense occurs only against a memory trace from an earlier phase that has not yet been translated. Repression is, therefore, within this model of the psyche, "a failure of translation"[28] caused through release of unpleasure generated by a translation. What is particularly important here is Freud's recognition of the power of repressed earlier memories—those that he designates as not having been successfully translated. Freud argues that what determines pathological defense or repression is the sexual nature of the event and its occurrence in an earlier phase. Herein, however, lies a problem with which Freud struggled over many years. Why repress sexual events given that they produce pleasurable excitations?

As a means of dealing with this problem at a proximate level[29] of explanation, Freud had begun to develop what was to become a very important psychoanalytic concept: the notion of deferred action. In this letter he argues that if an event A aroused unpleasure when current, then the registration of it, AI or AII, has a means of inhibiting the release of unpleasure when the memory is reawakened. Freud proposed that this suggests that the more the memory recurs, the more inhibited does the release become. There is a problem, however, in the case of sexual events. Here inhibition does not occur when memory recurrence brings greater release of unpleasure over time because, according to Freud, magnitudes of the excitations that these release increase with time because of sexual development. The details of this problem do not directly concern us here, but the link between repression and sexuality remained a core issue for Freud, and the idea of deferred action has continued to hold a pivotal position in Freudian theory and practice.

Conclusion

The Freud-Fliess correspondence contains within it two of Freud's four attempts to schematize the human psyche. The very observation that these schemas are found within such a context places constraints upon the nature of the formulations that they might contain. These letters and drafts were not only those of friend to friend but also from one medically minded man to another. Thus, the schemas are ones presupposing a shared knowledge base by both writer and reader—that of the medical sciences. It was not until 1900 when Freud proposed his third schema that he broke away from such an ostensibly neurological-physiological model. Although the Freud-Fliess correspondence continued until 1904, Masson's research about this time is illuminative. It was around 1900 when it became undeniably evident that Freud and Fliess had taken different and irreconcilable theoretical paths. Masson's discovery of an unpublished paper by Fliess, which quotes from a Fliess-Freud letter, provides evidence that by then Fliess firmly held to the idea that there was no need for Freud to work at psychotherapy because a patient became better or worse according to strictly biological periods.[30] Consequently, Freud needed to find a different and, it was hoped, receptive audience for his psychological hypotheses which were alien to a Fliessian approach. This, as we will see, led to his producing a less-limiting contextually constrained formulation.

Given that Freud was working on the basis of a physiological-neurological model of the mind, he unquestioningly adopted the assumptions of that discipline. This meant in effect that there was no question to be asked about the nature of human agency, but an assumption was made pertaining to the ultimate explanatory mode—one that assumes evolutionary causation. This is particularly clear in his theorization about the concept of repression.

Freud never asked who represses or why. What he was interested in was why the individual represses memories of a sexual nature. In search of an answer, he eventually moved to the ultimate level of explanation. This level underpins many of his theoretical ideas and allows him to bypass the problem of conceptualizing individual agency with its complicating factor of repression.

Irrespective of the already-noted theoretical and personal differences between Freud and Fliess, Freud's clinical practice took him into a field of experience that was entirely unknown to Fliess. Fliess had never listened to a patient's unconscious speech as had Freud, thus he was limited not just by a theoretical disposition but by different experiences as well. This means that Freud as clinician had to be a theoretician of a unique clinical practice—one for which in many ways he, too, was ill prepared. Within the parameters of his own practice he found it difficult to handle at a theoretical level those problems that faced him by unconsciously driven yet consciously willing human subjects. Now alone, Freud attempted to reconcile theory and practice in a slowly emerging new framework of conceptualization, one removed to some degree from the neurological-physiological framework found in the Freud-Fliess correspondence.

3

The First Topography:
The Third Schema

When Freud's major work, *Die Traumdeutung,* was published, it was clear that his conceptualization of the human psyche was in the process of undergoing a radical change. Whereas the first two attempts were built upon a neurological basis, the schema found in *The Interpretation of Dreams* was built on a developing psychological basis. It is important to note, too, that whereas the first two schemas were produced with one reader immediately in mind—namely, Fliess—*The Interpretation of Dreams* was read by Fliess before it went to press but was written with a general readership in mind.

Freud mentions his dream study throughout his correspondence with Fliess. On March 15, 1898, he writes: "The idea occurred to me that you might like to read my dream study but are too discreet to ask for it. It goes without saying that I would have sent it to you before it goes to press." [1] A copy of the book was sent to Fliess before October 27. Dreams had become of immense importance to Freud in view of his following his patients' associations, which were often interpolated with dream accounts. In addition, he carried out his own self-analysis at the same time as he wrote this work—thus the selection of his own analysis as exemplifying his theoretical propositions. On November 10, 1897, he wrote to Fliess that he wanted to write the book as a means of getting out of a bad mood: "But I also envy you because once again I do not know at all where I am and am bored with myself. I shall force myself to write the dream(book) in order to come out of it." [2]

The Interpretation of Dreams was published on November 4, 1899, but the publisher put the date 1900 on the title page. E. Jones[3] reports that 600 copies of the book were printed. It took eight years to sell them, with 123 copies sold in the first six weeks and 228 in the next two years. Ten years later a second edition was requested; there were eight editions in all during Freud's lifetime.

The Third Schema

In chapter 7 of *The Interpretation of Dreams,* Freud presents a number of hypotheses concerning the mental apparatus. His principle postulation, after Gustav Fechner, is that *"the scene of action of dreams is different from that of waking ideational life."*[4] This difference must be clearly acknowledged at the outset of this presentation because this schema is one that Freud devolved to account for dreams, not to account for everyday life as we experience it consciously. Freud's interest in chapter 7, "The Psychology of the Dream-Processes," is in the realm to which the dream can be attributed, namely, the unconscious. Here Freud is very careful to prevent the reader from equating the unconscious with any anatomical locality and suggests a possible analogy with a microscope or telescope:

> I shall remain upon psychological ground, and I propose simply to follow the suggestion that we should picture the instrument which carries out our mental functions as resembling a compound microscope or a photographic apparatus, or something of the kind. On that basis psychical locality will correspond to a point inside the apparatus at which one of the preliminary stages of an image comes into being. In the microscope and telescope, as we know these occur in part at ideal points, regions in which no tangible component of the apparatus is situated. I see no necessity to apologize for the imperfections of this or any similar imagery.[5]

Now, rather than talk in neurological terms, Freud presents a model of psychical agencies or systems, "ψ systems" (note the influence of the "Project"), which, although in order, are so perhaps temporally but not necessarily spatially. These systems compose the psychical apparatus and are depicted in diagram 3. Psychical processes move in general from the perceptual to the motor end (M). Clearly this is again, as in the first two schemas, a reflex apparatus: "Reflex processes remain the model of every psychical function."[6]

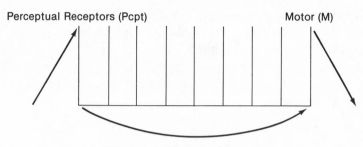

Diagram 3: The Third Schema (1)

In this new attempt to schematize the mind Freud notes the necessity for the apparatus to cope with two functions: (1) to retain modifications of the elements in the system (memory); and (2) to remain perpetually open to the reception of fresh modification. He therefore proposes two systems: (1) a system for the reception of stimuli—this system has no memory; and (2) a system that transforms excitations into permanent traces. We can see here a shadow of his earlier conceptualization in the "Project." Here, as in the letter of December 6, 1896, there are several mnemic systems (diagram 4), with the first system recording memories according to simultaneity in time and later systems arranging perceptual material according to similarity. The perceptual receptors retain no memory trace.

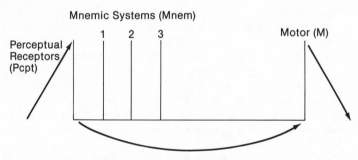

Diagram 4: The Third Schema (2)

The formation of dreams, Freud argues, can only be explained by hypothesizing agencies—"one of which submitted the activity of the other to a criticism which involved its exclusion from consciousness. The critical agency . . . stands in a closer relation to consciousness than the agency criticized: it stands like a screen between the latter and consciousness."[7] Using the notion of systems, Freud locates the critical system at the motor end of the apparatus. In addition to Pcpt., memory, and motor discharge or consciousness, Freud proposes another system at the motor end called the preconscious—the processes entering the preconscious can, under certain conditions, enter consciousness. The preconscious (Pcs.) system holds "the key to voluntary movement."[8] Diagram 5 shows the apparatus schematically.

Behind the Pcs. system is the unconscious (Ucs.), which has no access to consciousness except via the preconscious. Freud proposed that unconscious processes cannot get through to consciousness without submitting to modification. It is basically from within the unconscious system that the impetus for dream construction is located—namely, the dream wish. Without going into full details here concerning the construction of dreams, Freud proposed that the dream wish, defined as "a current in the apparatus starting from unpleasure and aiming at pleasure"[9] sets in motion a process called the dream work. This process involves (a) the primary processes—mentioned in neurological terms in the "Project"—designated as condensation and displacement and (b) the secondary processes concerning the possibility of representing the dream thoughts in some form, at times symbolically. The process of regression is also very important, for it is this process that allows for the hallucinatory quality that dreams possess. Between the two systems, that is between the latent and manifest content contained within them respectively, there is a censorship in operation; repressed wishes belong to the first system, and it is these wishes that the second system opposes. In terms of chronological priority, an important aspect with regard to development, there is no psychical apparatus that possesses primary processes only. Such an idea is a theoretical fiction. Nevertheless, Freud postulated that primary processes are

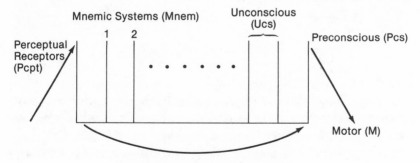

Diagram 5: The Third Schema (3)

present in the mental apparatus from the first, whereas only during the course of life do secondary processes unfold to inhibit and overlay the primary ones.

There are now, for Freud, three main psychical systems: the unconscious, the preconscious, and the conscious. A critical agency or censorship lies like a screen between the unconscious and the preconscious, modifying any excitatory process passing through to consciousness. This schema[10] of the apparatus is known as the first topography and was Freud's working model of the mind until after 1915 when he began to make the first moves toward his later second topography of 1923.

Freud's proposal is very confused at this point with regard to the notion of censorship within this third schema of the mind. For example, he identifies "the critical agency with the agency which directs our waking life and determines our voluntary, conscious actions."[11] This means that the preconscious acts as censor. Later he writes: "Experience shows us that this path leading through the preconscious to consciousness is barred to the dream-thoughts during the daytime by the censorship imposed by resistance." Freud holds that "there is a lowering of the resistance which guards the frontier between the unconscious and the preconscious"[12] and that is how dream-thoughts obtain access to consciousness. It is unclear, therefore, where the censor stands and how it operates or more particularly who operates it. Is it between the unconscious and preconscious or between the preconscious and consciousness? Who performs the censorship—the subject or the apparatus? In this schema of the mind, Freud does not acknowledge the idea of the subject, and—given his taken-for-granted assumptions concerning the agency of aspects of the apparatus— he fails to recognize the implied separation that he makes between agency and subject within the theory he expounds.

Agency

Certainly throughout *The Interpretation of Dreams* Freud attributes agency to the psychical systems themselves. Because nothing reaches consciousness from the first system without passing a second agency, it is this second agency that exercises its rights and makes modifications "as it thinks fit in the thought which is seeking admission to consciousness."[13]

In an early chapter, Freud describes one of his own dreams and explains the notion of censorship as follows:

> In just the same way my second agency, which commands the approaches to consciousness, distinguished my friend R. by a display of excessive affection simply because the wishful impulses belonging to the first system, for particular reasons of their own or whilst they were intent at the moment, chose to condemn him as a simpleton.[14]

We are led to understand that each agency has a mind of its own and that Freud himself suffered his dream or was indeed dreamed by the dream. In other passages, Freud more explicitly argues his case by homunculus analogy:

> Thus the censorship between the Ucs. and the Pcs., the assumption of whose existence is positively forced upon us by dreams, deserves to be recognized and respected as the watchman of our mental health. Must we not regard it, however, as an act of carelessness on the part of that watchman that it relaxes its activities during the night, allows the suppressed impulses in the Ucs. to find expression, and makes it possible for hallucinatory regression to occur once more?[15]

By now we can see that Freud presents both a structural or topographical account of the mind plus a functional account of the dynamic involved between the systems. In addition it is to be noted how he calls in the use of analogy to argue a case that is very, very difficult to express in its own terms. As Freud later says: "Analogies, it is true, decide nothing, but they can make one feel more at home."[16] How to handle the notion of censorship was a problem, but toward the end of *The Interpretation of Dreams* Freud had come to a point where he introduced the notion of a censorship between the preconscious and unconscious as well as one between the preconscious and consciousness. This introduction does in some sense overcome the noted contradictory or confusing descriptive statements referred to earlier.

The Concept of Repression in The Interpretation of Dreams

By 1900 Freud was using a number of terms to conceptualize at a theoretical level what he faced with the *hystérique d'occasion*, the problem of counter-will. Now, with respect to dreams, Freud talks in terms of censorship rather than defense but does assume that latent dream thoughts pertain to what has been repressed by the dreamer. This means that Freud utilizes the notion of clinical resistance and the concepts of repression and censorship to describe the dynamics of the mental apparatus. When he talks of psychical repression in particular, he veers very much toward his early neurological account except that, whereas in the earlier account of the psyche the dynamics were based on the principle of inertia, they are now based on the pleasure principle. This change was in all probability informed by his clinical experience. Thus, with specific reference to dreams, repression is described as the avoidance of a memory, a distressing mnemic image, which is itself a repetition of the previous flight from the perception. Freud also points out that unlike the perception, memory lacks the quality necessary to excite consciousness. Thus it cannot attract a fresh cathexis to itself: "This effortless and regular avoidance by the psychical process of the memory of anything that had once been distressing affords us the prototype and first example of *psychical repression*." [17] Here Freud provides the beginning of his dynamic account of repression, one that reached fulfillment in his 1915 paper which will be discussed in a later chapter. But here, in *The Interpretation of Dreams* the importance of the concept of repression to Freudian theory is beginning to emerge. Whereas earlier Freud could not cope with the concept, he was now working with it as the cornerstone of his theory of dreams, influenced very much by his theory of neuroses although he would have preferred this to be otherwise: "Nevertheless I am constantly being driven to do so." [18]

Freud's grappling with the notion of the split in the human subject between what the person wants or wills and what arrives without invitation had led him to postulate the concept of the unconscious. He is now in a position to claim that "the core of our being" consists of unconscious wishful impulses: [19]

> The unconscious is the larger sphere, which includes within it the smaller sphere of the conscious. Everything conscious has an unconscious preliminary stage; whereas what is unconscious may remain at that stage and nevertheless claim to be regarded as having the full value of a psychic process. The unconscious is the true psychical reality . . .[20]

The link between this description and the process of repression is integral to his theory both of the neuroses and of dreams. What is censored out of dreams is that which is repressed. The repressed are those wishes whose expression would bring unpleasure to the subject. In line with this theory of neuroses these wishes, at base infantile, pertain to the area of sexuality:

> Among these wishful impulses derived from infancy, which can neither by destroyed nor inhibited, there are some whose fulfillment would be a contradiction of the purposive ideas of secondary thinking. The fulfillment of these wishes would no longer generate an effect of pleasure but of unpleasure; and *it is precisely this transformation of affect which constitutes the essence of what we term "repression."* The problem of repression lies in the question of how it is and owing to what motive forces that this transformation occurs; but it is a problem that we need only touch upon here.[21]

Freud explains, and we can see the influence of the letter of December 6, 1896, here, that repression is successful when the generation of unpleasure ceases with the withdrawal of cathexis from the transference thoughts in the preconscious. Transference thoughts convey the unconscious wish. If repression is unsuccessful, symptom formation occurs. This means that thoughts force their way through to the preconscious. Herein begins a battle of defense—"for the Pcs. in turn reinforces its opposition to the repressed thoughts (i.e., produces an anticathexis)—and thereafter the transference thoughts, which are the vehicles of the unconscious wish, force their way through in some form of compromise which is reached by the production of a symptom.[22]

What was initially a problem of will versus counter-will has now been described in terms of will/symptom with the explanatory concepts of the unconscious, repression, and primary and secondary processes all used as intervening variables. The problem remains, nevertheless, as to the role of the subject within the context of the processes described. How are these processes linked to the individual whom Freud studied—the one who speaks within the analytic session?

The Dreamer in Relation to Dreams

In *The Interpretation of Dreams* Freud uses the concept of "ego" to designate a representation of the dreamer's self—"All of them are completely egoistic: the beloved ego appears in all of them, even though it may be disguised"[23]—as well as the agent that plays a role in producing the state of sleep: *"Thus the wish to sleep (which the conscious ego is concentrated upon, and which, together with the dream-censorship and the 'secondary revision'*

which I shall mention later, constitute the conscious ego's share in dreaming)
. . ."[24] It is as if the dreamer wishes to sleep but simultaneously does not
want to know his or her deepest thoughts and feelings. Because of persons' ability to censor dreams, even while asleep, they remain at a distance
from their true or unconscious thoughts. For example, Freud explains the
sensation of inhibition of movement in dreams as evidence of a conflict in
will. The unconscious purposes require the movement to go on, but the
censorship demands that it be stopped.

The problem of the relationship between the analytic subject and his
or her thoughts confronted Freud daily in his practice. Here he used
concepts such as the ego repressing sexuality to explain the nature of
symptom formation. However, his schema of the psyche presented in *The
Interpretation of Dreams* did not contain a representation of the ego as
such, only three agencies: conscious, preconscious, and unconscious. This
discrepancy between theory and practice was overcome in regard to the
concept of resistance which Freud formally theorized as repression, now
spelled out in some detail but without attention to the relationship between the conscious subject and his or her thoughts. All processes, as
described by Freud, are at this point devoid of a subject; they simply
operate within the subject—the latter suffers them. It is only the wish
that is needed, and the link between the subject and his or her wish is
never made at a theoretical level. Is the wish simply a current of energy?
What brings one person to wish one thing and another to wish something
very different? What is the link between what we think we wish and what
we might unconsciously wish? It is clear that this very issue troubled
Freud because, in 1919—that is, eighteen or nineteen years later—he felt
the need to add a footnote concerning the relationship between the
dreamer and his/her dreams. Once more, at a descriptive level, he argues
by homunculus analogy. Freud stresses the point that the subject is divided in the sense that the dreamer has no knowledge of his/her deepest
wishes as represented in the dream. Yet, if the dreamer does not know
his/her dreams, why does s/he censor them?

> No doubt a wish-fulfillment must bring pleasure; but the question then
> arises "To Whom?" To the person who has the wish, of course. But, as we
> know, a dreamer's relation to his wishes is a quite peculiar one. He repu-
> diates them and censors them—he has no liking for them, in short. So that
> their fulfillment will give him no pleasure, but just the opposite; and
> experience shows that this opposite appears in the form of anxiety, a fact

that has still to be explained. Thus a dreamer in his relation to his dream-wishes can only be compared to an amalgamation of two separate people who are linked by some important common element.[25]

Rather than develop this point further, Freud refers the reader to a familiar fairy tale concerning the moral that if two people are not at one with each other the fulfillment of a wish of one of them may bring nothing but unpleasure to the other. From the clinical perspective, Freud describes the subject in psychoanalysis as a divided subject but cannot account for "the important common element" that amalgamates him or her. From a theoretical point of view this division is accounted for by means of the divided psychical systems, but the relationship between the subject and the apparatus is never attended to from a theoretical perspective. What this means is that the gap between theory and practice had the potential of widening had it not been for Freud's strength in allowing clinical experience to inform theory construction. The footnote cited above is a case in point; here Freud draws attention to the problem presented for the concept of the pleasure principle in handling the clinical experience of nightmares and of punishment dreams. If dreams are to be wish fulfillments, then how does one account for the wish for experienced anxiety which can only be said to be unpleasurable? Freud suggests that with anxiety dreams the "satisfaction at the fulfillment of the repressed wish may turn out to be so great that it counterbalances the distressing feelings attached to the day's residues"[26]—the day's residues forming part of the manifest content of the dream construction. Furthermore, he argues: "Or it may happen that the sleeping ego takes a still larger share in the constructing of the dream, that it reacts to the satisfying of the repressed wish with violent indignation and puts an end to the dream with an outburst of anxiety."[27] If this is the case then Freud postulates an active, potent ego even while the dreamer dreams. Such a postulation contradicts the notion of a consciousness that is simply the recipient of unconscious processes that have found their way through the preconscious to consciousness. Where is this active ego in the schema? Freud has, it seems, two conceptual frameworks in operation: one clinically informed via his work with psychoneuroses and the other a theorization that is no doubt important in its contribution to dream theory yet at this stage is still inadequate. The problem of punishment dreams highlights this seeming contradiction in his formulations.

Punishment dreams are those dreams that the subject deals out in punishment to him/herself on account of an unconscious wish: "What is fulfilled in them is equally an unconscious wish, namely, a wish that the dreamer may be punished for a repressed and forbidden wishful impulse."[28] Although this wish for punishment is unconscious, Freud argues that "it must be reckoned as belonging not to the repressed but to the 'ego.' "[29] He acknowledges the problem as follows:

> Thus punishment-dreams indicate the possibility that the ego may have a greater share than was supposed in the construction of dreams. The mechanism of dream-formation would in general be greatly clarified if instead of the opposition between 'conscious' and 'unconscious' we were to speak of that between the 'ego' and the 'repressed.' This cannot be done however without taking account of the processes underlying the psycho-neuroses and for that reason it has not been carried out in the present work. . . .[30]

The problem noted in reference to the lack of correspondence between the third schema, Ucs., Pcs., Cs., and the ego versus the repressed formulations leads Freud to suspect that all that is unconscious is not simply "the repressed." In brief, Freud hints here at the possibility of an unconscious ego:

> The essential characteristic of punishment-dreams would thus be that in their case the dream-constructing wish is not an unconscious wish derived from the repressed (from the system Ucs.), but a punitive one reacting against it and belonging to the ego, though at the same time an unconscious (that is to say, preconscious) one.[31]

A footnote added in 1930 points out that this would be the appropriate point for reference to the super-ego. This concept will be discussed in the next and following chapters.

Freud acknowledged, in this first publication of his theory of the unconscious, that he was trying to conceptualize an "unknown reality."[32] He underlined that it was incorrect to look upon the systems as localities but that his terminology encouraged such an understanding—words such as "to repress," "to force through." It is not that a thought moves from one locality to another, a topographical notion, but more that "some particular mental group has had a cathexis of energy attached to it withdrawn from it, so that the structure in question has come under the sway of a particular agency or been withdrawn from it."[33] This alternative economic conceptualization places a different emphasis upon the systematic description of the psychical apparatus and its functioning. The need to offer this alternative way of presenting the theory underscores the efforts that Freud was willing to put into his theorization and the difficulties involved in adequate conceptualization. It is as if he attempted and reattempted to present alternative hypothetical propositions to deal with what always eluded his grasp. This, his third schema of the mind, had provided fuller understanding of the psychical processes and the differences between them than his earlier schemas; it allowed Freud to develop a fuller explanation of repression but, at the same time, produced problems in regard to a lack of correspondence between the concept of the ego and the notion of the system consciousness. At the heart of this outcome was a failure that beset Freud from the outset: he never clarified his theoretical assumptions regarding the nature of human agency. As a consequence, his theorization and his clinical experience brought him to an impasse. We will see now how he once more attempts to deal with this impasse, though yet again fails to clarify his position regarding the subject in psychoanalysis.

Conclusion

At the origin of his attempts to schematize the psyche Freud worked on the basis of the taken-for-granteds of the medical sciences. This meant that the concept of agency was irrelevant within the terms of the "Project" and the letter of December 6, 1896. Similarly, neither then nor later did he give cognizance to the question of how the subject in psychoanalysis might be conceptualized. Thus, rather than provide a theory of the psychoanalytic subject, Freud rectified or re-presented his schemas of the psychical apparatus without ever questioning the taken-for-granteds that provided the basis of his theoretical propositions. As a consequence of this omission, Freud deals with the problem of agency by means of (a) incorporating an explanatory homunculus analogy that itself contained the concept of agent; (b) reverting to a basically neurological or energy-bound explanation that requires no agent but rests on the premises of the medical sciences; or (c) simply imputing agency to the systems themselves. One may well suspect that Frank Sulloway is correct when he argues that Freud was a biologist at heart and that Strachey is correct in saying about Freud that "he certainly never gave up his belief that ultimately a physical groundwork for psychology would be established."[34]

Certainly, as late as 1916–17, Freud states in the *Introductory Lectures*: "The theoretical structure of psycho-analysis that we have created is in truth a superstructure, which will one day have to be set upon its organic foundation. But we are still ignorant of this."[35]

This being so, it seems that Freud's subject is no more than an organism with psychological processes, simply built on the premise of the reflex arc. Yet somehow a reading of the *Standard Edition* does not allow such a definitive statement about the Freudian subject. The Freudian subject is a subject who is divided in terms of will and unconscious wish. What a reading of the first five volumes of the *Standard Edition* does allow is the argument that Freud was held back in his theorization by the nature of his unchallenged assumptions. He was held back from taking as his starting point the psychoanalytic subject who acts and speaks in accordance with what is willed, yet who both dreams and falters in subjective expression for reasons beyond the realm of commonsense knowledge.

4

The Metapsychology: A Crisis Point

The Context

It was not until 1915 that Freud turned once more to the difficult task of grounding his growing clinical experience in soundly expounded psychological theory. In the interim he had published a great deal, including his renowned work the *Three Essays on the Theory of Sexuality;*[1] his well-documented clinical case histories "Dora,"[2] "Little Hans,"[3] and "The Rat Man";[4] a refutation of dissensions, *Totem and Taboo;*[5] and the "Papers on Technique."[6]

One important paper contributing to Freud's theoretical stance was his 1911 "Two Principles of Mental Functioning" in which he elaborates upon the notion of the pleasure principle and the reality principle associated with the primary and secondary processes, respectively. Within this paper Freud suggests a change in the development of the ego, but he remains unclear about this point. Here he talks in terms of two egos— one associated with pleasure, the other with reality—and hints at a progression from one stage to the next: "Just as the pleasure-ego can do nothing but *wish,* work for a yield of pleasure, and avoid unpleasure so the reality-ego need do nothing but strive for what is *useful* and guard itself against damage."[7] He later writes: "While the ego goes through its transformation from a pleasure-ego into a reality ego . . ."[8] suggesting a progression. Irrespective of the problem of a lack of clarity, what this paper points to is Freud's growing interest in the notion of the ego apart from its repressive function as had been the case earlier. Freud was now working on the idea of development taking two courses: one with regard to the ego and the other with regard to the sexual instincts.

The war years themselves were among the most productive in the history of Freud's psychoanalytic contributions. Jones reports that, while speaking to Sandor Ferenczi about some of his new ideas, Freud indicated that he was feeling the effects of his own political situation: "Now I am more isolated from the world than ever, and expect to be so later too as the result of the war. I know that I am writing for only five people in the present, you and the few others. Germany has not earned my sympathy as an analyst, and as for our common Fatherland the less said the better."[9] The people mentioned were Karl Abraham, Ferenczi, Otto Rank, Hanns Sachs, and Ernest Jones—all analysts who conversed closely with Freud. This means that the metapsychological papers he produced at this time had one type of reader in mind: those who knew Freud's work intimately and those who had sympathy for his views.

Produced in the years 1914–18, these papers are of a very high standard, which puts them out of reach of the general interested public. They are the work of an analyst for analysts. Freud's papers were to be published in the *Zeitschrift (Internationale Zeitschrift für Psychoanalyze),* the first number of which appeared in 1913. During the war years Freud worked extremely hard to keep the then-current journals in circulation: "After all, we wish to keep the journals alive at all costs while the war lasts and to conduct them in such a way that later we shall be able to produce them with pride."[10] Freud, who was then in his sixtieth year, wanted to produce a complete and comprehensive description of many mental process and to do so wished to include three aspects: an account of (1) the dynamic attributes, (2) the topological features, and (3) the economic significance. The term covering all three is the concept "metapsychology." In a period of seven weeks Freud produced five papers, which, according to Jones, "are among the most profound and important of all Freud's works."[11] These papers—"Instincts and Their Vicissitudes," "Repression," "The Unconscious," "The Metapsychological Supplement to the Theory of Dreams," and "Mourning and Melancholia"—were followed by seven others, which were never published. The latter were probably destroyed by Freud; it seems that they dealt with Consciousness, Anxiety, Conversion Hysteria, Obsessional Neuroses, and the Transference Neuroses in General. Sublimation and Projection may well have been the other two titles.

As argued in the previous chapters, in 1900 Freud was employing two conceptualizations of the psychical apparatus in conflict with itself. In simplest terms, these may well be designated as the clinical model—ego versus sexual instincts—and the first topographical model—Ucs., Pcs., Cs. It is the argument of this chapter that the metapsychological papers were a pivotal crisis point in Freud's theorization. Which of the above conceptualizations would become the basis of further endeavor? If Freud chose the former, then the ego was a concept requiring much fuller elucidation because it was, at least implicitly, imputed with the agency of the individual. If the latter conceptualization were chosen, then the agency of the individual, be that by implication, was imputed to the system unconscious. As a means of investigating the direction chosen by Freud, these five papers will be explored to discover where Freud imputed the notion of agency within the formulation and which conceptualization was thereby implied.

"Instincts and Their Vicissitudes"

By 1915 Freud had moved away from his medical-scientific conceptual framework to a newly emerging territory: the psychological. Nevertheless, he was still tied to the assumptions of his prior perspective. The movement to the psychological with its residue from the past is clearly indicated in his definition of an instinct:

> If now we apply ourselves to considering mental life from a *biological* point of view, an "instinct" appears to us as a concept on the frontier between the mental and the somatic, as the psychical representative of the stimuli originating from within the organism and reaching the mind, as a measure of the demand made upon the mind for work in consequence of its connection with the body.[12]

The drive or instinct belongs to neither the somatic nor the mental and is best understood as a psychical representative.

In 1910 in a paper "Psychogenic Disturbances of Vision"[13] Freud introduced the idea of "ego-instincts." These had two components: (1) self-preservative instincts and (2) a repressive function. Thus in his 1915 paper he reminds his reader that he has proposed two groups of primal instincts to be distinguished as the ego, or self-preservative instincts, and the sexual instincts. Importantly for the present argument, Freud goes on to point out that this supposition does not have the status of a necessary postulate but, rather, that it is merely a working hypothesis "to be retained only so long as it proves useful, and it will make little difference to the results of our work of description and classification if it is replaced by another."[14] He explains that the hypothesis arose in the course of the evolution of psycho-analysis, which was first concerned with the transference neuroses (hysteria and obsessional neurosis) and, it was these that showed that at root there was always "a conflict between the claims of sexuality and those of the ego."[15] For the present, he writes, we have not met "with any argument unfavorable to drawing this contrast between sexual and ego-instincts."[16]

Clearly, Freud based this paper on the ego-versus-sexuality model, in which case his overall supposition is that, generally speaking, the ego has control over sexual instincts. At times this is not so, and consequently a neurosis develops. With "Instincts and Their Vicissitudes" Freud develops the concept of the ego along expectable lines such that the ego is placed within a developmental framework and given active attributes. In brief, the ego develops from the stage of autoeroticism to object choice; and what was the original "reality-ego," which distinguished between internal and external, changes into a "pleasure-ego," which places the characteristic of pleasure above all else. This latter ego develops into the final reality-ego. Freud talks of the agency of the ego in terms of introjecting and projecting objects into and out of itself and of hating and loving. He writes, for example:

> The ego hates, abhors and pursues with intent to destroy all objects which are a source of unpleasurable feeling for it . . .
> Love is derived from the capacity of the ego to satisfy some of its instinctual impulses auto-erotically by obtaining organ pleasure.[17]

Love and hate pertain, not to the instincts and their objects, but to "the relations of the *total ego* to objects."[18] The sexual instincts, on the other hand, undergo various vicissitudes in the process of their development, namely: reversal into the opposite (e.g., love into hate) and turning around upon the subject's own self (e.g., masochism from sadism, repression, or sublimation).

Two points regarding Freud's instinct theory must be dealt with very briefly here. First, after many alterations, Freud came to the conclusion that there are two basic instincts: *Eros* and the destructive instinct. The former refers to that drive that aims "to establish ever greater unities and to preserve them . . . to bind together"; and the aim of the latter, namely the death drive, is "to undo connections and so to destroy things."[19] We will see that Melanie Klein bases much of her theory on these drives. Whereas for Freud they are conceived at the ultimate level, Klein employs them at the proximate level. Second, in early Freud, drives were understood to pertain to the biological notion of bodily energy; they were forces toward a particular direction. In the *Three Essays* Freud introduced the concept of *Trieb,* which was a concept found (see p. 57) "on the frontier between the mental and the somatic." By the time Freud employed the notion of the life and death instincts (1920), drives had come to include the libido theory of 1915, to be briefly explained in the next paragraph, and cosmic notions as well.

It is clear from the preceeding discussion that Freud relied solely upon the clinical model in his paper on instincts. The notion of the first topography was neither required nor drawn upon at any point. Furthermore, although built on a premise of conflict, the ego rather than the sexual instincts is imputed with the upper hand. However, with the introduction of the concept of narcissism in 1914, Freud unwittingly introduced complications into his theoretical postulations. The ego instinct of self-preservation was then to be regarded as narcissism or self-love, with the result that instead of a conflict between ego instincts and sexual instincts Freud had produced the conceptual impossibility of a conflict between two libidos: ego libido and sexual libido. This meant that all was libido. To deal with the theoretical impasse, Freud postulated a nonlibidinal component of the ego which was referred to as self-interest. He held that there were ego and object instincts other than libidinal ones, but he arrived finally at the 1920 proposition of the conflictual conceptualization in terms of *Eros* versus the death instinct. This means, then, that Freud maintained a clinical model but moved it into a dynamic/economic account away from the topographical conceptualization necessitated by the Ucs., Pcs., Cs. schema.

"Repression"

In his 1914 paper "On the History of the Psycho-Analytic Movement" Freud made the point that "the theory of repression is the corner-stone on which the whole structure of psycho-analysis rests."[20] Later, in his *An Autobiographical Study* (1925) he wrote similarly: "It is possible to take repression as a centre and to bring all the elements of psycho-analytic theory into relation to it."[21] In previous chapters of this book we saw how quickly the concept of repression and its importance to psychoanalysis were recognized by Freud. It is not surprising, therefore, that in his first public lectures delivered at Clark University in Worcester, Massachusetts, (1909) Freud spoke of repression to the everyday person. There, much in keeping with his clinical model, he talked about wishful impulses that are incompatible with ethical and aesthetic standards of a person's personality. He explained the concept using the analogy of a lecturer sending a noisy person outside (repression) and how that gentleman might form a resistance to expulsion by banging on the door. He states somewhat succinctly: "Thus the incompatibility of the wish in question with the patient's ego was the motive for the repression; the subject's ethical and other standards were the repressing forces."[22] At this stage and given his audience, Freud provided a description of repression that was underpinned by a consciously active subject. The assumption is that repression could well be an intentional act given the analogy, but need not necessarily be so.

However in 1915 Freud, writing for his most knowledgeable and skilled analysts, provides a decisively critical paper on the theory of repression. By this time he had used the concept in two ways: either as synonymous with defense so that in the "Rat Man" case of 1909, written for those familiar with the field of psychoanalysis,—and so named owing to the patient's obsessive fear concerning the sadistic use of rats—he described the displacement of the emotional cathexis from the objectionable idea[23] or at other times as meaning the complete expulsion of the idea from consciousness, as in hysteria. In the 1915 paper he refers to the latter type of repression.

Because of the importance of this concept to the notion of the Freudian subject, it is important to look carefully at the translation from the

German. The 1915 paper's title in German is *"Die Verdrängung,"* which "in essence consists only of the rebuff or a keeping at a distance from the conscious."[24] According to Bettleheim, the difference between the German and English words is that the German implies an inner urge. Furthermore, topography is not implied. This is clear when one goes to the root of the German. *Verdrängung* is derived from the word *Drang,* which is explained by the example "to give in to a strong inner motive." "A *Verdrängung* is thus a displacement or dislodgement caused by an inner process. The German word gives no indication in which direction such dislodging or pushing away takes place."[25] Bettleheim makes the revealingly important point that the exact German equivalent of the English word *repression* is *Unterdrückung,* which literally means "squeezing under." Freud did not use this term. Both *suppression* and *repression* used as translations of *Verdrängung* indicate a direction, whereas the correct translation of the noun *Verdrängung* is "repulsion" and of the verb *verdrängen,* "to repulse".

The 1915 text itself corresponds in essence to the Bettleheim translation, for Freud writes that "the essence of repression lies simply in turning something away, and keeping it at a distance from consciousness."[26] There is no hint of direction. However there is mention, as in earlier papers, that repression is not a defensive mechanism present from the beginning but one that arises when there is a cleavage between conscious and unconscious. Freud then presents the important concept of primal repression, the first stage of repression. Primal repression, which is a theoretical assumption, consists in a psychical representative of the instinct that is being denied entrance into the conscious. A fixation is established, which means that the representative in question persists in an unaltered form from then onward. Repression proper, the second stage of repression, effects the mental derivatives of the originally repressed representative and other trains of thought that have come into association with it. Freud elaborates on a critical theoretical issue from the point of view of his underpinning assumptions concerning the location of agency:

> Moreover, it is a mistake to emphasize only the repulsion which operates from the direction of the conscious upon what is to be repressed; quite as important is the attraction exercised by what was primarily repressed upon everything with which it can establish a connection. Probably the trend towards repression would fail in its purpose if these two forces did not co-

operate, if there were not something previously repressed ready to receive what is repelled by the conscious.[27]

Agency is attributed, therefore, to both a pull and a push; but who exerts these forces, and why, remains undisclosed. Although Freud acknowledges that repression acts in a highly individual manner, the assumption is that it does act rather than that the individual actively represses. It does not seem to be a case of "either-or" but rather a case of "and"—that is, that the subject is repressed *and* that the subject represses.

Much detail is provided about the life of repressed instinctual representatives and their derivitives and associations—how they develop, organize themselves, and establish new connections. Energy is needed not just once; a continual energy is required to keep the repression successful. The fate of a repressed instinctual representative is a threefold possibility: (1) it may remain successfully suppressed so that no trace is found; (2) it may appear as an affect that is in some way qualitatively colored; or (3) it may be changed into anxiety. In his earlier work, Freud maintained that repressed sexuality was converted into the form of anxiety; but in 1923 he altered this theory, proposing that it was anxiety that produced repression. The importance of this change is that it releases the concept of repression from its sexual bondage. Anxiety may be produced from situations that are associated with other meanings. Although that change did not take place until 1923 and although Freud did delineate the different form of repression found in the psychoneuroses, this paper on repression certainly addresses repression proper rather than pathological repression, which Freud always connected with sexuality. As he clearly states: "We recall the fact that the motive and purpose of repression was nothing else than the avoidance of unpleasure."[28] Unpleasure may be derived from countless espoused value systems that have been transgressed or situations causing psychological pain.

The difficulty in theorizing about the concept of repression is, as Freud points out, that "the mechanism of a repression becomes accessible to us only by our deducing that mechanism from the *outcome* of the repression on the ideational portion of the representative, we discover that as a rule it creates a *substitutive formation*. . . . Further we know that repression leaves symptoms behind it."[29] Irrespective of this difficulty, Freud provides a brilliant account of the mechanism of repression. Given that this paper follows that on instincts, one may well assume that Freud was working on the basis of the conceptualization of the ego versus sexual instincts though he does refer to the conscious-unconscious schema throughout the discussion—for example, "the repulsion which operates from the direction of the conscious upon what is to be repressed"; [30] and "Repression in fact interferes only with the relation of the instinctual representative to *one* psychical system, namely, to that of the conscious." [31] Here both the clinical and the topographical models are utilized at the same time.

The concept of repression, as presented, could well be employed within either of Freud's models. Furthermore, it seems to provide a bridge or connecting tissue between two logically mutually exclusive topographies as far as the notion of agency is concerned. Repression is a dynamic or a mechanism inherent within both descriptions of the psychical apparatus. Yet, as always, Freud takes no account of the relationship, at a theoretical level, between this cornerstone concept and the subject in psychoanalysis. It is interesting that even though Freud is writing for his most well versed of analysts, he nevertheless felt the need to use his ever-present homunculus analogy to clarify a point concerning whether an idea is held back or has vanished from consciousness: "The difference is not important; it amounts to much the same thing as the difference between my ordering an undesirable guest out of my drawing-room (or out of my front hall), and my refusing, after recognizing him, to let him cross my threshold at all." [32] The problem with this analogy is that Freud is the one doing the expelling. In his discussion of repression, however, there is no subject— just processes unattached to any agent.

"The Unconscious"

The paper on the unconscious is the culmination of the metapsychological series. Following 1900, Freud published two papers specifically focused on the concept of the unconscious: "Two Principles of Mental Functioning" (1911) and "A Note on the Unconscious' (1912) [33] although, of course, there are countless references to and dealings with the unconscious throughout his other works. The paper on the unconscious is divided into seven sections, each of which will be briefly mentioned.

Freud begins with an argument to justify the concept of the unconscious. He states at the outset that "the repressed does not cover everything that is unconscious. The unconscious has the wider compass: the

repressed is a part of the unconscious."[34] He follows this introduction
with a section on the topographical point of view in which he raises the
problem of adequate conceptualization. Again, as in 1900, he emphasizes
that "our psychical topography has *for the present* nothing to do with
anatomy; it has reference not to anatomical localities, but to regions in
the mental apparatus, wherever they may be situated in the body."[35] This
topographical account of the processes does bind Freud to the idea of
space and regions so that two-dimensional representations always seem
applicable for descriptive purposes. Yet, it is this very notion that he tries
to do away with. In the midst of this section, Freud raises a question
concerning the adequacy of the topographical conceptualization—Is there
a change of place or a change of state in an idea that is transposed from
the system Ucs. into the system Cs. (or Pcs.)?

> are we to suppose that this transcription involves a fresh record—as it were,
> a second registration—of the idea in question, which may thus be situated
> as well in a fresh psychical locality, and alongside of which the original
> unconscious registration continues to exist? Or are we rather to believe that
> the transposition consists in a change in the state of the idea, a change
> involving the same material and occuring in the same locality?[36]

After some discussion Freud concludes that he is not in a position at this
stage to decide between the two possibilities. He even goes so far as to
say "Perhaps we shall make the discovery that our question was inade-
quately framed and that the difference between an unconscious and a
conscious idea has to be defined in quite another way."[37] I shall return to
this point when dealing with section seven, where such an attempt is
made in relation to speech.

The third section of the paper discusses the problem of unconscious
emotions. Freud argues that in theory there are no unconscious affects as
there are unconscious ideas but that in practice we do use the term. He
follows this section with a further exposition of the topography and
dynamics of repression based solely on the first topography and relying
on the assumption of neurology for the transmission of "excitations."
This means, of course, that he does not need to consider the subject
involved. Rather, as often, he imputes agency to the system or process
itself, bypassing the need to mention the analytic subject:

> Soon the same mechanism finds a fresh application. The process of repres-
> sion, as we know is not yet completed, and it finds a further aim in the task

of inhibiting the development of the anxiety which arises from the substitute . . .[38]

Section five provides a clear delineation of the characteristics of the
unconscious: exemption from mutual contradiction, primary process,
timelessness, and the replacement of external by psychical reality. These
are of the utmost importance to clinical work and are almost certainly
derived from this source.

Perhaps the most fraught with difficulties is the section headed "Communication Between the Systems." Here, the real problem between the
conceptualizations is brought into relief. Not only does Freud acknowledge a discrepancy between the postulation of distinct regions of the
mind and what is found in clinical practice, but he also argues his case to
an interesting point. First, he points out that the Ucs. is continued into
what is known as derivatives, that it is accessible to the impressions of
life, that it constantly influences the Pcs. and can even be subjected to
influences from the Pcs. He recognizes that this contradicts the expectations of "a schematically clear-cut distinction between two psychical
systems"[39] but argues that there is no obligation for him to produce at
first attempt a well-rounded theory that commends itself by virtue of its
simplicity. He endorses, in this section, the idea of two censorships as
hinted at in *The Interpretation of Dreams*—a censorship that is decisive for
becoming conscious between the systems Ucs. and Pcs. and the probability of a censorship between the Pcs. and Cs. This is important in that,
because every transition from one system to another corresponds to a new
censorship, then the assumption of a continuous laying down of new
registrations is not necessary. Because this discussion centers on the third
schema or first topography of the psychical apparatus which, as we have
seen, rests on the assumption of the potency of the unconscious, Freud
defines "being conscious" in terms of a symptom. This, of course, is the
logical outcome of adopting this schema, one that places great importance
on the concept of the unconscious. "Being conscious" is relegated to the
status of "symptom":

> The more we seek to win our way to a metapsychological view of mental
> life, the more we must learn to emancipate ourselves from the importance
> of the symptom of "being conscious."[40]

Toward the end of this section Freud employs the concept of the ego
and inserts the idea of the possibility of the unconscious being "ego-

syntonic." It is as if he cannot manage at a theoretical level without this concept, which is the nearest to the experienced conscious-I. On the one hand "being conscious" is a symptom, whereas on the other hand it is possible for the unconscious to be ego-syntonic. It does seem that the unpalatable notion is watered down, via a different model, to something more easily digested.

The Unconscious and Speech

Given that psychoanalysis is above all else a discipline that relies on and works with human speech, it is somewhat surprising that it is not until section seven of the 1915 paper that Freud discusses the connection between speech and his theory.[41] We will return to this theme of psychoanalysis and language in later chapters. In this section, entitled "Assessment of the Unconscious," Freud links his psychoanalytic theorizing with his preanalytic work of 1891 on aphasia.[42] Here Freud attempts to draw a distinction between the transference neuroses and narcissistic problems by an investigation of the schizophrenic's use of speech. He points out that in schizophrenia words are subjected to the same process as that which makes dream images out of the latent dream thoughts, that is to the primary processes. Because these words undergo condensation and displacement, they transfer their cathexes to one another in their entirety. This means that in schizophrenia object cathexes are given up and the cathexes of word presentations maintained. Freud then theorizes on the basis of the third schema within the context of understanding the nature of dreams. He is still concerned with his topographical argument and arrives at a very different conclusion:

> The two are not, as we suppose, different registrations of the same content in different localities, nor yet different functional states of cathexes in the same locality; but the conscious presentation comprises the presentation of the thing plus the presentation of the word belonging to it, while the unconscious presentation is the presentation of the thing alone. The system Ucs. contains the thing-cathexis of the objects, the first and true object-cathexis; the system Pcs. comes about by this thing-presentation being hypercathected through being linked with the word-presentations corresponding to it.[43]

Now, instead of neurological excitations or the sheer transcription of mnemic images, Freud has moved to a conceptualization that is grounded in speech. Thus, as hinted at earlier, he attempts to define the psychical apparatus quite differently. We will see the importance of this direction later where it is argued that the unconscious is best defined in the light of one's theory of the subject in psychoanalysis—namely, the subject who speaks to the analyst. For Freud at this point, the third schema is by implication defined in terms of its link with speech: for example, "As we can see, being linked with word presentations is not yet the same thing as becoming conscious, but only makes it possible to become so; it is therefore characteristic of the system Pcs. and of that system alone."[44] Repression, too, is redefined within the appropriate terms: "Now, too, we are in a position to state precisely what it is that repression denies to the rejected presentation in the transference neuroses: what it denies to the presentation is translation into words which shall remain attached to the object."[45] The influence of schema two can also be seen here.

Although Freud did refer again to this type of conceptualization[46] the lost paper on consciousness may well have been very illuminating here. Although Freud was well prepared to theorize from a neurological perspective, he was not equipped to venture ahead from within the field of linguistics. Yet, the paper on the unconscious indicates that it is from within the latter domain that theory development may have been undertaken. Ferdinand de Saussure's posthumous *Course in General Linguistics*[47] was published in 1915, and Freud could have drawn upon it later if he had wished. Furthermore Freud wrote a preface to Raymond de Saussure's *La methode psychanalytique*[48] in 1922. Raymond was the linguist's son and himself a psychoanalyst. This suggests a possible close contact for Freud with a linguistic vein of thought. However, as we will see, Freud remained within the arena of the metapsychology he had hoped to produce. Consequently, because the assumptions he had made inadvertantly were never challenged, he continued to work within a framework of the medical sciences, constrained by the reflex model that it assumes.

"The Metapsychology of Dreams"

"The Metapsychology of Dreams," written in 1915, was not published until 1917. In essence this paper is an application of Freud's attempt to provide a topographic, dynamic, and economic description of chapter 7 of *The Interpretation of Dreams*. The main discussion, however, is one that concerns the problem of hallucination and how it is that in our normal state of mind we are able to differentiate between fantasy and reality. Once more, Freud is involved, albeit unwittingly, with the problem of choice of conceptualization. Here the discussion revolves around a key issue within the present argument: namely, the problem involved in utilizing two models or conceptualizations that are based on irreconcilable theoretical assumptions concerning the notion of human agency. In this paper Freud returns to much that was discussed in the "Project," in particular, with an emphasis upon the function of the ego in distinguishing between an idea and a perception. When discussing the problem of discriminating between what is internal and what is external in the light of the third schema which is employed in this paper, Freud proposes:

> The Cs. must have at its disposal a motor innervation which determines whether the perception can be made to disappear or whether it proves resistant. Reality-testing need be nothing more than this contrivance. We can say nothing more precise on this point, for we know too little as yet of the nature and mode of operation of the system Cs. We shall place reality-testing among the major *institutions of the ego,* alongside the *censorship* which we have come to recognize between the psychical systems . . .[49]

The lost paper on consciousness would again be invaluable here. Without it Freud seems beholden to the concept of the ego to handle the problems that he faces. Throughout the metapsychological papers Freud makes it clear that his theory, with all the complexities that it is endeavoring to explain about the mental life of human beings, requires both conceptualizations simultaneously. Just as he was able to propose in the paper on the unconscious that it is a general truth that our mental activity moves in two opposite directions—from the instincts, through the system Ucs. to conscious thought activity or from the outside, through the system Cs. and Pcs. to Ucs.—so, too, does he make clear that he requires both the third schema and his clinical model to take into account the multiplicity of psychological events that he attempts to explain.

"Mourning and Melancholia"

Like its predecessor, the paper "Mourning and Melancholia" was written in 1915 but was not published until 1917. Apart from its immense clinical importance, the significance of this paper within the present context lies in its work on the concept of the ego and its consideration of a critical agency already alluded to in the first topography.

In discussing the distinction between mourning and melancholia, Freud describes the clinical features in terms of a difference in loss: in mourning, it is the world that becomes poor and empty; in melancholia, it is the ego itself that has become poor and empty. Freud explains this latter phenomenon of the melancholic's self-rejection in terms of a particular constitution of the ego. Here, we need to refer back to his 1914 paper "Narcissism," where Freud proposed the concept of the ideal ego. The latter refers to the idea that individuals set up in themselves an ideal against which they measure their actual ego. Because, in the 1914 paper, repression proceeds from the ego, Freud states: "For the ego the formation of an ideal would be the conditioning factor of repression."[50] Furthermore, Freud theorizes that what individuals put before themselves as ideal is the substitute for the lost narcissism of childhood in which the individual is its own ideal. This led to the further proposition of "a special psychical agency which performs the task of seeing that narcissistic satisfaction from the ego ideal is ensured and which, with this end in view constantly watches the actual ego and measures it by that ideal."[51] The super-ego of the second topography to be discussed in the chapter to follow is a combination of this agency and the ego ideal. Now, in "Mourning and Melancholia," Freud suggests that one part of the ego sets itself against the other, and by taking it as its object, judges it critically: "What we are here becoming acquainted with is the agency commonly called 'conscience.' "[52] Freud proposes that conscience, along with the censorship of consciousness and reality testing, is among the major institutions of the ego. The unique clinical feature of melancholia is not simply the employment of the agency of conscience, but in addition the identification of one part of the ego with the lost object so that one part of the ego bears down upon the other, which is now identified with the abandoned object:

> In this way an object-loss was transformed into an ego-loss and the conflict between the ego and the loved person into a cleavage between the critical activity of the ego and the ego as altered by identification.[53]

What is so important in this formulation is that the ego can become, at least in part, an object to itself. It can be both subject and object as in the "Project." Furthermore, this formulation, as with the concept of narcissism, is based on the clinical model of ego versus sexual instincts; but in both papers, the concept of the ego is developed beyond its simple repressive function. In other words, in these papers, the ego takes a central place and offers itself as a potentially focal point for ongoing theory construction.

Conclusion

The five papers on metapsychology, written in a short period during the war years, emerge in the works of Freud as a crisis point. Although these papers contain some of Freud's deepest theoretical propositions with regard to man's psychical life, they also contain a fundamental dilemma found throughout his theory construction. The metapsychological papers are a thorough and richly rewarding endeavor to hypothesize with the greatest possible purchase about the realm that can only be known by its effects—namely, the unconscious. These papers expose Freud at his best, but they also expose the problem that beset his conceptual scaffolding—a failure to address his work on the basis of known assumptions. Because he never acknowledged the theoretical assumptions underpinning his attempts to conceptualize the psyche, Freud found that he needed two mutually exclusive formulations to cope with the problem that he faced in both theory and practice.

Owing to his use of these models, one clinical and the other topographical, Freud's theory construction is embedded with contradictory assumptions concerning the location of the concept of agency. Furthermore, that Freud did not proffer a theory of the subject in psychoanalysis led him to develop a schema of the psychic apparatus unattached to any notion of the subject. The way in which Freud developed a second topography will be the focus of the chapter to follow.

5

The Second Topography:
A Compromise Solution

A Problem to Be Faced

In 1923 Freud addressed the problem that involved an attempt to reconcile a clinically derived model, with one type of assumption about the
agency of the subject, with a theoretically formulated schema based on a
logically incompatible assumption about the agency of the subject. This
problem as presented in the previous chapter was explicitly mentioned in
Freud's 1920 work *Beyond the Pleasure Principle*.[1] When discussing the
clinical observation of the analysand's resistances, Freud points out that
these resistances are unconscious and that this raises a problem as far as
terminology is concerned:

> We shall avoid a lack of clarity if we make our contrast not between the
> conscious and the unconscious but between the coherent *ego* and the *re-
> pressed*. It is certain that much of the ego is itself unconscious, and notably
> what we may describe as its nucleus; only a small part of it is covered by the
> term "preconscious." Having replaced a purely descriptive terminology by
> one which is systematic or dynamic, we can say that the patient's resistance
> arises from his ego, and we then at once perceive that the compulsion to
> repeat must be ascribed to the unconscious repressed.[2]

The importance of the ego within Freud's theorization became increasingly clear when in 1921 he published *Group Psychology and the Analysis of
the Ego*[3] Here he discusses the concept of identification in some detail,
explaining the process within the terms of the Oedipus complex. The

metapsychological description is complex and difficult and is not of immediate relevance other than its focus upon the work of the ego and in its paving the way for a needed revision of the first topography, which could no longer serve practical purposes. In summary, Freud needed a new topographical model of the mind because:

1. as early as 1900, in *The Interpretation of Dreams,* Freud noted the role of the ego in producing punishment dreams. This ego, of course, was assumed to be unconscious (see pp. 51–52);
2. in his 1914 paper "Narcissism" and his 1915 paper "Mourning and Melancholia," Freud proposed the notion of the ego ideal and a self-critical agency that watched over the ego measuring it by that ideal (see pp. 68–69);
3. in his clinical experience he had observed both the effect of unconscious guilt and the unconscious resistance of the ego (see p. 19).

This meant that although it was incorrect to equate the ego with the conscious and the preconscious and the repressed with the unconscious, it was also clear that there was a need to postulate another dynamic agency, the super-ego, representing the postulations of the critical agency and the ego ideal. In an attempt to cope with this dilemma Freud wrote *The Ego and the Id* (1923),[4] in which he proposed his second topography or fourth schema. This book was written with a large readership in mind because by this time Freud's work was known internationally. Indeed, in September of 1922, the seventh International Psycho-Analytical Congress had been convened in Berlin. It was here that Freud read a short paper entitled "Some Remarks on the Unconscious,"[5] which foreshadowed the work of his later book.

The Ego and the Id

The Ego and the Id and its tripartite presentation of the mind has become a popularized version of Freudian theory. However, one cannot help being struck by the implicit warning contained in Freud's words to Ferenczi with reference to the publication: ". . . and the present book is decidedly obscure, composed in an artificial fashion and badly written . . . Except for the basic idea of the 'Id' and the aperçu about the origin of morality I am displeased with really everything in the book."[6] In this work Freud attempted to encompass the best of both worlds. He tried to include the richness of his third schema, which rests upon the assumption of the power of the unconscious. His aim, in addition, was to include his clinically derived model, one that rests upon an opposing assumption concerning the potency of the ego. Consequently, this second topography or fourth schema is not only obscure but, as Freud himself admits, poorly written. This criticism can be made on the grounds that Freud, in attempting to combine two incompatible schemas, has produced a hybrid form. Subsequently, description of this hybrid can only eventuate in a contradictory or confusing publication. This is not to suggest that *The Ego and the Id* fails to be a worthwhile theoretical contribution. It is to suggest, nonetheless, that, as always, Freud's omitting to deal with the assumptions underpinning his theory construction led him to postulate a topography of the mind that, in the long run, may well have given rise to the possibility of losing much that was radical and revolutionary in his contribution to our understanding of the subject in psychoanalysis. The consequences of his neglect will be discussed in the chapters to follow.

Freud sums up the argument of *The Ego and the Id* when he writes: "We shall now look upon an individual as a psychical id, unknown and unconscious, upon whose surface rests the ego, developed from its nucleus the Pcpt. system."[7] Although he does discuss the concept of the super-ego it is interesting that it is not included in his topographical schema until that provided in the *New Introductory Lectures* of 1933.[8] It is in fact the ego that claims much of his attention in this work—particularly its function and its relationship with the two other components of the psychic apparatus. Diagram 6 is the schema depicting the second topography, which will now be discussed.

The Pcpt.-Cs. represents a system that Freud uses to differentiate among external perception, memory, and hallucination. Sensations and feelings are also discussed in relation to this system. Freud queries if it is correct to refer the whole of consciousness to this topographically superficial system, because there is a theoretical problem—which does not concern us—with regard to the notion of "unconscious feelings." The influence of his earlier second schema is clearly apparent in this particular system of the 1923 schema. The "Acoust." relates to an aspect of the apparatus that concerns verbal residues which are derived primarily from auditory perception.

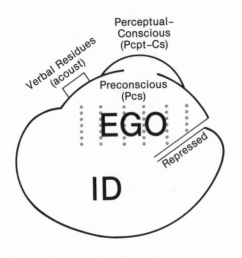

Diagram 6: The Fourth Schema

Reminiscent of the ego of the "Project," Freud explains that in each individual there is an ego, a "coherent organization of mental processes."[9] This ego is attached to consciousness and controls the approaches to motility. Its function as a mental agency is to supervise all its own processes and, although it goes to sleep at night, it nonetheless even then exercises censorship on dreams. It is the ego of the fourth schema that, as has been the case throughout, is the operative force in repression. Within the terms of this schema the ego is undoubtedly a potent mental constituent. Freud describes it as formed to a great extent out of identifications and as part of the id, which has been modified by the direct influence of the external world through the medium of the Pcpt.-Cs. system. Not only does the ego influence conscious activity but it also seeks to bring the influence of the external world to bear upon the id. It "endeavors to substitute the reality principle for the pleasure principle which reigns unrestrictedly in the Id."[10] What is referred to as reason and common sense is represented by the ego whereas, in contrast, the id contains the passions. From the topographical point of view, the ego does not completely envelop the id but only to the extent that the system Pcpt. forms the ego's surface. There is no sharp delineation between the ego and the id: the ego's lower portion merges into the id. This allows for the necessary notion of the unconscious ego, one of the driving forces in producing this new schema. The ego is ultimately derived from bodily sensations and is best regarded as a mental projection of the surface of the body.

When describing the relationship between the ego and the id, Freud once more calls upon an analogy, the famous rider and horse. The ego

> is like a man on horse-back, who has to hold in check the superior strength of the horse; with this difference, that the rider tries to do so with his own strength while the ego uses borrowed forces. The analogy may be carried a little further. Often a rider, if he is not to be parted from his horse, is obliged to guide it where it wants to go; so in the same way the ego is in the habit of transforming the id's will into action as if it were its own.[11]

Here again, Freud is bothered by the problem of will, of psychical agency. From a functional point of view, Freud imputes considerable potency to the concept of the 1923 ego; but, simultaneously, his id has strong and determining effects. This time, Freud describes the battle of wills as between man and horse, but even after almost thirty years of experience a problem of willpower emerges surreptitiously. Both ego and id, via the analogy, are conceived as possessing a will be they at odds or in line with each other. The point that the ego, unlike the rider, has to borrow its strength from an undesignated elsewhere, suggests that it is the id that has the greater strength. We have yet to see the position of the ego in relation to the super-ego. What is clear, however, is that the id has lost the immense richness of the 1915 "unconscious." The id is now the reservoir of the libido and the wellspring of passion: a horse to be tamed.

The Super-Ego

The super-ego, not represented on the present schema, is a concept introduced by Freud after many years of flirting with its components: the idea of a self-critical, unconscious agency and the establishment of an ego ideal. Freud notes that it would be vain to attempt to localize the ego ideal but does so in the schema of the *New Introductory Lectures* (see p. 83). In brief, Freud explains the development of the super-ego as follows. In the beginning, object-cathexis proceeds from the id; then, when the ego develops, it sets up within it both the abandoned and current object-cathexis of the id. Individuals vary in their capacity later to resist the influence of such object-cathexes. The origin of the ego ideal finds its place in childhood—it is the identification that the child makes with its parents. This is not the result of object-cathexis as such but is very early identification. A later-cathexis reinforces this primary identification, and it is this later object-cathexis that is central to the problem of the resolution of the Oedipus complex.

Without going into detail with regard to this very involved matter, suffice it to say that the super-ego is "heir of the Oedipus complex and thus it is also the expression of the most powerful impulses and most important libidinal vicissitudes of the id."[12] As heir it is comprised of the identification with the parents' own super-egos. Once set up, the super-ego has a particular relation with the ego: "By setting up this ego ideal, the ego has mastered the Oedipus complex and at the same time placed itself in subjection to the id."[13] This means that the ego as representative of the external world stands in contrast to, and is criticized by, the superego, the representative of the internal world. From the topographical point of view, the superego is close to the id: it can act as its representative with regard to the ego. The super-ego is further from consciousness than the ego and, rather than being separate from the id, reaches deep down into it. The relationship between the ego and the super-ego is one of tension. It produces the commonly experienced sense of guilt, but in the instances of obsessional guilt, melancholic guilt, and hysterical guilt the nature of the relationship is more complex but need not bother us here.

What is of importance now, however, is to recognize the position of the ego with respect to both the id and the super-ego. As Freud writes: "Helpless in both directions, the ego defends itself vainly, alike against the instigations of the murderous id and against the reproaches of the punishing conscience."[14] This means that the potent and active ego as described earlier is also the ego of subjection; it is both strong and weak. It is strong in its position with regard to the processes of thinking and reality testing and to its control over motility: "in the matter of action the ego's position is like the constitutional monarch without whose sanction no law can be passed but who hesitates long before imposing his veto on any measure put forward by Parliament."[15] The ego is also weak in that it is "a poor creature owing service to three masters."[16] This service is to the demands of the critical super-ego, of the libidinal id, and the external world.

When describing the ego as a "frontier-creature," Freud uses two of his constant theoretical ploys: he either imputes agency to the construct being discussed or utilizes a homunculus analogy. Not only does he depict the ego in its weakness, but also yet again displays the weakness of his theoretical position in his second topography. Having never reconsidered his premises he reconceptualizes the psyche without adequately dealing with the problems of agency or the subject in psychoanalysis. The following quotation is an example *par excellence* of Freud's position:

> As a frontier-creature, the ego tries to mediate between the world and the id, to make the id pliable to the world and, by means of its muscular activity, to make the world fall in with the wishes of the id. In point of fact it behaves like the physician during an analytic treatment: it offers itself, with the attention it pays to the real world, as a libidinal object to the id, and aims at attaching the id's libido to itself. It is not only a helper to the id; it is also a submissive slave who courts his master's love. Whenever possible, it tries to remain on good terms with the id; it clothes the id's Ucs. commands with its Pcs. rationalizations; it pretends that the id is showing obedience to the admonitions of reality, even when in fact it is remaining obstinate and unyielding; it disguises the id's conflicts with reality and, if possible, its conflicts with the super-ego too. In its position midway between the id and reality, it only too often yields to the temptation to become sycophantic, opportunist and lying, like a politician who sees the truth but wants to keep his place in popular favor.[17]

The new agencies, superimposed upon the old topography of the third schema so as to cope with the inadequacies found in clinical practice, gave Freud his fourth schema. This schema marks a shift in emphasis, from one focused on the unconscious to one focused on the ego. From 1900 on Freud was particularly concerned with the theory of the unconscious, as can be evidenced from the great papers of the metapsychology. From 1923 on, however, it is evident that ego theory constantly troubled him from a theoretical perspective. This is not surprising because, as Laplanche argued that the ego was neither subject nor an object in Freud's "Project," so too is the ego simultaneously active and passive in *The Ego and the Id*. Before considering Freud's post-1923 work on the ego, which continually demonstrates this theoretical impasse, translation problems with specific reference to the second topography require our attention.

The "I," the Above "I," and the It

It has been argued that in *The Ego and the Id* Freud continued to weaken his theoretical propositions by virtue of his neglect to address adequately the problem of human agency. In the light of Bettleheim's thesis that Freud has been poorly translated, it could be argued that the real issue is one of lost meaning rather than failure at a theoretical level.

Bettleheim points out that where the German *Ich* is translated as "ego" there is a loss of the sense of the personal commitment that we make when we say "I" or "me." Were the translation "I" made, then Freud's theories would be brought closer to the reader and to the deep personal meaning that Freud intended. According to Bettleheim *Ich* refers to that I which can often be employed assertively as an image of how a person's I "tries to assert its will over what in the translations are called the "id" and "superego" and over the external world." [18] *Das Ich* refers primarily to the conscious, rational aspects of oneself, to an organization of the soul that is interpolated between the stimulation of the senses and the perception of the individual's bodily needs as well as motor acts. Although Bettleheim argues that we recognize that this "I" is not the fullness of the apparatus of the soul, there is also another region, "more extensive, grander, and more obscure than the I, and this we call the it." [19]

Before investigating the "id" translation it is important to note the significance with which Bettleheim invests *das Ich*. He claims that when Freud names the conscious, reasonable aspects of our mind the I, he is referring to what we value most highly in ourselves—"our real I":

> It gives us the intuitive feeling that Freud is right to name the I what we feel to be our true self, even though we know that we do not always act in line with that self. [20]

This translation which insists on the value and supremacy of the "I" is precisely in line with the theoretical assumption underlying the introduction of the concept into the second topography. Yet, in *The Interpretation of Dreams* where Freud utilized the first topography it is clear that he holds a contradictory view—namely, that "the core of our being" is unconscious. Surely the core is more likely to be related to the notion of our true self?

Nevertheless, if we accept Bettleheim's proposal, the "id" requires

reconsideration as well. The id, from the German *das Es,* is better translated as "the it," but the latter does not carry the full emotional impact of
the original German. In German the phrase *das Es* carries the sense of
childhood, of how the reader was referred to *(das Kind)* before he learned
to repress his sexual, aggressive, and otherwise asocial impulses. It brings
to mind the time before the individual felt guilty or ashamed, before there
was the need to resolve contradictions or to bring logical order into
thought—"in short, it reminds him of a time when his entire existence
was dominated by the it."[21] In addition to personalizing these two concepts, Bettleheim's translation personalizes the superego as well. Rather
than taking the super-ego to be an overbearing and unknown threat to
the individual, Bettleheim suggests that *Über-Ich* is best understood as the
above-I with an emphasis placed upon the second part of the concept to
underscore that the *Über-Ich* is an integral part of the person. This emphasis is to be made in an attempt to communicate the idea that

> it is the person himself who created this controlling institution of his mind,
> that the above-I is the result of his own experience, desires, needs and
> anxieties, as they have been interpreted by him, and that this institution
> attained its role of power because he, the person, internalized in its contents
> the demands he made—and continues to make—of himself.[22]

What in effect Bettleheim's translation does is to bring a deeply personal element into a seemingly mechanical and soul-less model. In some
sense, we could say that Bettleheim tries to introduce the notion of the
subject in psychoanalysis but does so at the level of discourse rather than
at the level of theory construction. What his argument does is to give
potency and significance to the conscious I without giving recognition to
the concept of the unconscious, which Freud had not really dispensed
with in his second topography. This discrepancy throws into relief what
has become a common tendency: to employ Freud's first topography or
his second one minus the first—that is, to employ the conceptual scaffolding of the conscious, preconscious, and unconscious or to employ the
ego, super-ego, and id terminology without acknowledgment of the schema
in its fullness, which is one that incorporates both the clinical and topographical models as described in the preceeding chapters.

The Fate of the Ego

Freud's interest in the ego did not cease with his second topography presented in *The Ego and the Id*. Not long afterward, in 1925, he worked on *Inhibitions, Symptoms and Anxiety*[23] which was published the following year. Again, the ego was of focal concern in his theory construction—this time with particular reference to the key concept of repression. Here, Freud proposes that inhibition is "the expression of a *restriction of an ego-function*"[24] and is brought about as a means of not having to employ repression. By renouncing certain functions, the ego can avoid conflict with both the id and the super-ego and so avoid repression and conse-quent symptom formation. Whereas earlier Freud had held that cathectic energy of the repressed impulses was automatically turned into anxiety, he now postulates that the ego is the actual seat of anxiety and sets repression in motion. Furthermore the ego is presented in all its strength: "Just as the ego controls the path to action in regard to the external world, so it controls access to consciousness. In repression it exercises its power in both directions, acting in the one manner upon the instinctual impulse itself and in the other upon the (psychical) representatives of that impulse."[25] Freud refers to what might seem an irreconcilable approach to the ego in viewing it as "the slave of three masters." In defense, he sits on the fence stating that one cannot take an extreme and one-sided view.

Freud discusses the problem of the ego, simultaneously strong and weak. He argues that the apparent contradiction is due to having taken the abstractions too rigidly and restates its topographical relationship with the id. He emphasizes that although the ego is distinct from the id and therefore weak, it is also bound up with and indistinguishable from the id, and therefore strong. The same is true in relation to the topography of the ego and super-ego: as a rule they are distinct, and a tension exists between them. Yet, in many situations the two are merged. In addition, although the ego is an organization that represses instinctual impulses, it is not all-powerful because the instinctual impulse that is to be repressed remains isolated.

The effect of repression, too, causes problems for the ego because the mental process that has been converted into a symptom owing to repres-sion now maintains its existence outside the organization of the ego and remains independent of it. This, it is to be noted, is a retheorization of will and counter-will after approximately thirty years of work. Rather than will we have the ego, and in place of counter-will we have the symptom. Freud goes further here and proposes a secondary defensive struggle carried out by the ego, where the ego tries to bind the symptom into its organization and so draws advantage from the symptom itself.

Freud endeavored to handle the problem that he saw with his simultaneously weak and strong ego by proposing a far more fluid and mobile topographical description of the psychical apparatus, one in which there are no hard lines but movement and merging between processes and organizations. A two-dimensional schema can never depict such a description: an issue that he mentioned in both *The Interpretation of Dreams* and his paper the "Unconscious" (1915). Freud was looking for a new topography, one that had potential purchase on an exceedingly difficult and complex theoretical conceptualization. As will become clear in the following, Freud reached such a proposal in the 1933 *New Introductory Lectures*. However, importantly for present purposes, a statement in *Civilization and Its Discontents* draws attention to Freud's adherence to his third schema, the first topography, and highlights the status of the ego when this schema is employed. Notably the ego's status is neither one of weakness nor of strength but as a charlatan in relation to the id:

> Normally, there is nothing of which we are more certain than the feeling of our self, of our own ego. This ego appears to us as something autonomous and unitary, marked off distinctly from everything else. That such an appearance is deceptive, and that on the contrary the ego is continued inwards, without any sharp delimitation, into an unconscious mental entity which we designate as the id and for which it serves as a kind of facade—this was a discovery first made by psycho-analytic research, which should still have much more to tell us about the relation of the ego and the id. But towards the outside, at any rate, the ego seems to maintain clear and sharp lines of demarcation.[26]

This presentation of the ego is one based on the underlying assumption that the true self is closer to the id than the ego and that is where potency lies. This is diametrically opposed to the assumptions of Bettleheim's translation of Freud's ego, super-ego, and id in which the I of consciousness is the true self. Furthermore this extract exemplifies Freud's use of the concept of ego as synonymous with the concept of self yet argues toward the contradictory idea that it is the unconscious or id that is closer to the true self. Such inconsistency is to be accounted for by Freud's omitting to clarify his theoretical approach to the notion of the subject in psychoanalysis.

From a conceptual point of view Freud's theorization is beset by two differing problems, both of which are fundamentally linked to the non-addressed problem of human agency. The first problem relates to inconsistent assumptions in the use of the conscious, preconscious, and unconscious and the ego, super-ego and id formulations; the second relates to a contradictory characterization of the ego as simultaneously strong and weak. As already indicated, Freud's answer was to readdress the topographical schema. Such an answer could never be highly productive. This is so because it does not bear on the real problem—namely, the need to acknowledge the theoretical underpinnings of his work.

The Final Schema

In 1930 Freud was honored with the Goethe prize for literature. The contribution that psychoanalysis had made to literature includes not only a series of journals but also its own publishing house founded in Vienna in January 1919, the Internationaler Psychoanalytischer Verlag. The history of the Verlag is a story in itself that is not important in the present context except to recognize that in 1932 its affairs were in a desperate state. As a means of helping to keep the Verlag afloat, Freud decided to write a second series of Introductory Lectures which would be a way of reporting the progress made since the first series fifteen years earlier: "Certainly this work comes more from a need of the Verlag than any need on my part . . ."[27] Whereas the *Introductory Lectures* were actually delivered, the *New Introductory Lectures* never were.

Within the seven lectures, one entitled "The Dissection of the Psychical Personality" bears a footnote to explain that the greater part of the material in the lecture is derived with some amplifications from chapters 1, 2, 3, and 5 of *The Ego and the Id*. In the opening paragraphs of the lecture Freud notes that the paper is to focus on the "ego of popular psychology," described as a "resisting, repelling, repressing agency."[28] Here he characterizes the ego as able to take itself as an object yet holds that in its very essence it is a subject. Thus he argues, "The ego can be split; it splits itself during a number of its functions—temporarily at least."[29] In theoretical terms, the process of the splitting of the ego was carried further forward by Freud in a posthumously published paper entitled "Splitting of the Ego in the Process of Defense."[30] In this clinically important paper Freud proposed that the act of disavowal resulted in a splitting of the ego. However, in the *New Introductory Lectures* Freud was writing for a broad public and not as a means of coming to terms with a theoretical notion. He was writing for the financial benefit of the Verlag, thus at a "popular" level.

As earlier, Freud works with the unconscious, preconscious, and conscious and the ego, super-ego, and id formulations. He mentions the ego's strengths and weaknesses and provides a diagram that is new in that his schema now includes the super-ego. This schema was printed upright in the original lectures but was turned onto its side in both the German editions of the complete works.

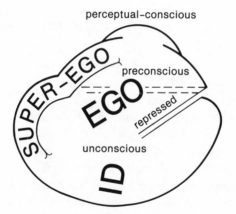

Diagram 7: The Final Schema

Freud explains that here the super-ego merges into the id and that it is more remote than the ego from the perceptual system. According to this diagram the id has intercourse with the external world only through the ego, but he states that it is difficult to say how correct the drawing is. The space occupied by the unconscious id ought to have been incomparably greater than that of the ego or the preconscious, as Freud explains. He goes on to again remove the sharp delineations that might be thought to exist between the agencies and systems, pointing out that rather than linear outlines areas of color melting into one another would provide a better pictorial description of "something so intangible as psychical processes."[31] It is clear that Freud is still, in 1933, moving toward a much more labile account of his schematization of the human psyche. To move in such a direction would demand a very different conceptual underpinning from what Freud had been employing in his two-dimensional presentations. It has been left to those who follow him to devise the means of reaping the rewards while enriching his theory with an adequate theoretical underpinning.

Otto Rank

I have argued that Freud began his psychoanalytic inquiry in the face of a subject whose willpower, or agency, presented a problem in everyday life. It is interesting to note in passing that Rank returns to this same issue in the sense that the concept of will is central to his non-Freudian proposals. His resolution of the problem of will, or the problem of failed efficacy of will, is one that differs radically from that which we have traced in the preceeding chapters.

Rank held that birth itself was the prototype of all later attacks of fear and that all mental conflicts concerned the relationship of mother to child. Thus he dispensed with a key Freudian concept, the Oedipus complex. Most importantly here, Rank claims that Freud deprived the personality of the very qualities that he himself held make man's life human: "autonomy, responsibility and conscience."[32] He argues that determinism "can never be the psychological answer to the human problem, because it denies the human phenomenon par excellence, the individual will."[33] In place of Freud's sexual etiology of the neuroses, Rank understands the neuroses as a result of an excessive control on the part of people's wills over their own nature: "The individual's will is either asserted in creation or lost in neurosis depending upon the individual's attitude towards this dilemma."[34] Will is a central concept for Rank, whose therapy aims at self-acceptance:

> By will, I do not mean will-to-power as conceived by Nietzsche and Adler or "wish" in the Freudian sense, though it might include both these aspects. I mean rather an autonomous organizing force in the individual which does not represent any particular biological impulse or social drive but consti-

tutes the *creative expression of the total personality* and distinguishes one individual from another. This individual will as the united and balancing force between impulses and inhibition is the decisive psychological factor in human behavior.[35]

Here we can see how the subject is expressed in and through agency.

Rank has moved his theory into the context of the everyday world of common sense rather than remain in the realm of psychoanalysis. His subject is not the subject who speaks to the analyst but the subject of the everyday world which fails to recognize and acknowledge the Freudian discovery of the unconscious and its effects.

Conclusion

It has been argued in this chapter that the second topography is a symptom of Freud's failure adequately to address the problem of human agency. This schema contains the superimposition of a clinically derived model containing the notion of an agent ego upon a more theoretically derived conceptualization of the mental apparatus which originated with *The Interpretation of Dreams*. Although the importance of both aspects of the compromise solution must be recognized within the framework of the history of Freud's psychoanalytic ideas, his theoretical scaffolding is undermined by a lack at the level of theoretical presupposition.

In sum, what this means with regard to the question of the subject and agency in psychoanalysis is that Freud's theory remains devoid of any clear explanation of either concept. Furthermore, I have shown that in the third and fourth schemas it is Freud's general tendency to impute agency to the apparatus. Because the apparatus is by implication distinct from the subject in his formulations, *Freud divides the concept of agency and the concept of the subject in psychoanalysis*. In his theory the status of the subject remains unaddressed, and it is the psychic apparatus itself that is imputed with agency even if that attribution is made at the expense of theoretical consistency. Thus, for Freud, although there may well be an unexamined underlying notion of the subject, his focus of interest is the psychic apparatus which is not the subject. We have, therefore, an implied separation between the subject and agency in Freud's theory. It should be mentioned here that Rank holds the concepts as integral to one another and thus employs them as undivided. He avoids the division between subject and agency and perhaps automatically moves out of the Freudian field.

The implicit but crucially important division between subject and agency has proved to be a core problem for psychoanalytic theory. How this is so will constitute the discussion of the chapters to follow. Two main problems ensue from the adoption of Freud's second topography of the psychic apparatus. First, theorists who take the second topography into their own theoretical contributions inevitably adopt Freud's contradictions and inconsistencies regarding the location of agency as shown in the foregoing chapters. This means that their theories ipso facto contain inherent logical impasses and problems of inconsistent and incoherent formulation. Second, what is also at stake is the nature of the assumptions made concerning the subject in psychoanalysis. Because Freud did not theorize on the notion of the subject, future theorists within the Freudian tradition have been left either to explicitly or implicitly develop their own particular perspective regarding the subject in psychoanalysis. This freedom has had major consequences for theory construction.

We will turn now to look at the work of those theorists who have, in varying ways, made a theoretical contribution to the psychoanalytic endeavor. We will see in particular how their contributions, being based on an adoption of Freud's second topography, are crucially influenced by the inherent separation between the concept of agency and the concept of the subject in psychoanalysis.

THE FREUDIAN LEGACY

6

A Problem Concerning the Subject in Psychoanalysis

Introduction

A number of psychoanalytic theorists have taken Freud's second topography unreservedly into their own theoretical considerations. Consequently, they have failed to interrogate the nature of their stance toward the notion of the subject and have, instead, worked toward the development of aspects of the topography, economics, and dynamics of the mind as postulated by Freud. Although these theorists may not have focused directly on the concept of the subject as an area for theoretical exploration, their work is underpinned by particular assumptions made concerning the subject in their psychoanalytic theory. What is important here is to bring into relief the possible differences in the assumptions made where theorists have taken the same Freudian schema into their work. The significance of seeing these differences is that this provides evidence of the consequence of the conceptual split between subject and agency in psychoanalytic theory. In particular we will see that in the case of both Heinz Hartmann and Melanie Klein, neither makes any assumption that necessarily or primarily concerns the subject who speaks to the analyst. This means that even though both work, at least initially, within the Freudian tradition by virtue of the schema that is basic to their hypotheses, these theorists make disparate assumptions concerning the concept of the subject. The subject, in each case, is perhaps best located in a domain other than that of the psychoanalytic enterprise.

At the outset of this chapter we will turn to the work of Anna Freud. Not only does Anna Freud provide an instance of the inheritance of problems for those who unquestioningly take Freud's schema into their work but she is also important in setting a direction for the work of Heinz Hartmann. We will turn, then, to question the nature of the assumptions made by Hartmann where the subject is concerned. It is my argument that Hartmann's subject is the subject in sociology and that this is to be accounted for by the nature of the question that he asks in his theoretical elaborations. Last, we will move to the work of Melanie Klein. Here we will see that the assumptions she makes concerning the subject in psychoanalysis are assumptions that pertain to an innately moral being. The theoretical conceptualization of the subject who speaks to the analyst remains to be found in the work of Jacques Lacan, whose contribution to psychoanalysis is the focus of the discussion in the chapter to follow.

Anna Freud

Foremost among those who have adopted Freud's schema of the mind is his youngest daughter, Anna. In 1922, the year prior to the publication of *The Ego and the Id,* Anna Freud was made a member of the Vienna Society, and in 1923 she entered analytic practice. An outcome of this practice was the appearance in 1927 of her first book, *Introduction to the Technique of Child Analysis,*[1] a work in which she described the differences between her approach and that of Melanie Klein, and some ten years later the publication first in German (1936) and then in English (1937) of *The Ego and the Mechanisms of Defense.*[2] It is this latter work that claims our attention here, particularly in reference to her use of Freud's second topography. Although there are eight volumes of her written work[3] I draw upon this work alone because it exemplifies the point that I wish to make with reference to the nature of the theoretical problems to be found where Freud's schema is adopted without question.

In *The Ego and the Mechanisms of Defense,* presented to her father on his eightieth birthday, Anna Freud argues a case from the basis of a clearly stated therapeutic stance. She makes the point very early in her book that although psychoanalysis in its earliest years of theory building was preeminently a psychology of the unconscious or the id, from a therapeutic point of view this is an inaccurate description of its intention:

From the beginning analysis, as a therapeutic method, was concerned with the ego and its aberrations: the investigation of the id and of its mode of operation was always only a means to an end. And the end was invariably the same: the correction of these abnormalities and the restoration of the ego to its integrity.[4]

It is from this therapeutic stance that Anna Freud develops her notions of the ego. This means, in effect, that her theory is a theory of therapy because she draws a clear distinction between the theory of psychoanalysis and the practical implementation of a clinical method. Whereas it has been argued that Freud was constantly reviewing his theory in the light of his clinical findings—hence he had a dialectical approach—Anna Freud takes a different path. Rather than have a theory inform her practice she takes the path of one whose practice informs a theory of the ego. It is not surprising, therefore, that Anna Freud places a particular emphasis upon technique.

From the outset she works on the basis of Freud's second topography which, as has been shown, incorporates both the first topography of conscious, preconscious, and unconscious with the introduction of the id, ego, and super-ego structures. It is the latter three institutions that claim her attention—in particular, the ego. The ego, however, refers to both the unconscious and the conscious psychic apparatus, but it is the former that is her major focus. This is so because she delineates and explores the unconscious defenses utilized by the ego in psychoanalytic therapy. It is her contention, in the light of her deliberations on the ego, that there are two stages in analysis: (1) the analysis of the ego; then (2) the analysis of the id. As a consequence of this position she portrays the ego in its defensive roles and puts into motion a clinical emphasis to be found in the ego school, the analysis of the resistance.

One of the most important shifts made by Anna Freud concerns her theoretical approach to the concept of repression. Whereas Freud's cornerstone was undoubtedly that of repression, Anna works on the basis of positing repression as one among a number of defenses employed by the ego. This means, in effect, that it is no longer the cornerstone of psychoanalytic theory but simply one among a number of bricks in the clinical edifice. This shift allows her to raise the other defenses such as denial, reaction formation, projection, and introjection to a higher status and so provides the ego with a battery of maneuvers to defend itself against the instinctual demand or what she terms pain. This rebalancing produces a theory of therapy where the ego is a central and potent agency whose livelihood is to be maintained. Her justification for the dethronment of repression is her claim that in 1926, in his work *Inhibitions, Symptoms and Anxiety* Freud refuted that repression occupies a unique position among the psychic processes. Anna Freud places great emphasis upon the analysis of these defenses and also upon the notion of the development of the ego. This is, of course, in keeping with her general thrust—the centrality of the ego.

Agency

Throughout her exposition, the ego is conceptualized in terms of one institution of the psychic personality. Without any clarifying definition of the concept itself, Anna Freud employs the notion of the ego as an institution endowed with effective agency. It is the ego that struggles against instinctual life; it is the ego that takes into account the orders of the super-ego: "The ego submits to the higher institution and obediently enters into a struggle against the instinctual impulse, with all the consequences which such a struggle entails.[5] Just as Freud imputed the apparatus with agency, so, too, does his daughter. Anna Freud simply adopted Freud's terminology and used it with her own particular therapeutic emphasis. At no stage does she question the assumptions made in using the structural terms "id," "ego" and "super-ego" and therefore subsumes within her own perspective those inconsistencies that have been elaborated on in the chapters on Freud's schemas. The effect of this failure can be seen in the form of the "license" that Anna Freud takes when describing her clinical cases. Here she shifts from the use of the terminology of the psychic apparatus to the use of the notion of the subject.

Whereas from a theoretical perspective it is the ego that is endowed with agency, from a clinical point of view she provides contradictory evidence. Sometimes it is the ego that bears the potency, at other times it is the subject. For instance, when writing of the restriction of the ego she says:

> When a child is somewhat older his greater freedom of physical movement and his increased powers of psychic activity enable his ego to evade such

stimuli and there is no need for him to perform so complicated a psychic operation as that of denial.[6]

Here both ego and child are imputed with agency. That may well be acceptable, but how the subject and ego are linked, if they are, is never referred to as a problem. This, of course, is an inheritance from Freud who, as we know, did not address the issue of how the subject in psychoanalysis might be conceptualized. Again she writes of a case as follows:

> He restricted the functioning of his ego and drew back greatly to the detriment of his development, from any external situation which might possibly give rise to the type of "pain" which he feared most.[7]

In this instance it is the subject who has command of the ego, be that the unconscious ego. Does this imply that the subject can utilize the psychic apparatus at will? Although this suggestion is quite contrary to the tenor of her work, one is left to speculate as to the implied link between ego or apparatus and subject and to the implied nature of agency, be that of the ego or subject, conscious or unconscious.

Clearly, there is need for further clarification surrounding the problem of both subject and agency in the work of Anna Freud. It would be inappropriate to expect *The Ego and the Mechanisms of Defense* to be a thoroughly thought-out theoretical framework because this was not her aim. However, given the fact that Anna Freud employed Freud's concepts, she adopted, without question, his failure to explore the theoretical underpinning regarding the notion of agency and the notion of the subject in psychoanalysis. Consequently her work holds unavoidable contradictions. Not only is Anna Freud's work important in its own right[8] and important as an example of one who has inherited the Freudian difficulty but it is also the influence of her work that has set a specific direction for later psychoanalytic theorization.

Hartmann, whose work we are to consider next, has taken Freud's concept of the ego, as did Anna, and developed this concept in a particular way. Throughout his work he acknowledges and accepts Anna Freud's contribution but broadens the concept of the ego beyond that of defensive agency. Hartmann endorses Anna's proposed centralized ego and to some degree authorizes his approach by placing his theoretical contribution within the light that Anna Freud shed on the character of the ego as agent.

Heinz Hartmann

Heinz Hartmann, regarded "as Freud's 'heir apparent' "[9] when he arrived in New York from Vienna in 1941, is best known for his work in the area of ego psychology. Hartmann's ego is that which is central within the terms of the structure of Freud's second topography and is a concept that derives much from the influence of Anna Freud. What is especially important in his work, within the present context, is that although he imports Freud's schema into his theory, he does not question the assumptions upon which it rests. Thus he automatically inherits problems with regard to an adequate conceptualization of agency and of the subject in much the same way as did Anna Freud. In addition, as a consequence of this neglect, Hartmann's theoretical perspective is based upon an implicit but particular notion of the subject in psychoanalysis. This subject, I argue, is the subject in the everyday world or the subject in sociology rather than the subject defined as the one who speaks to the analyst. That Hartmann can theorize on the basis of such a theoretical assumption is a legacy of the division found in Freud's concepts of agency and subject. Agency and subject are divided in Freud's theory, and both concepts are open to a variety of conceptualizations by later theorists working in the Freudian tradition. In the case of Hartmann, the notion of agency is Freudian in the sense that, like Freud, Hartmann imputes it to the psychic apparatus. The notion of the subject, however, is unique to Hartmann's ego psychology and is derived from the type of question that underpins his endeavor. It is to this question that we now turn our attention. We will see that because Freud did not adequately specify and conceptualize the notion of the subject in psychoanalysis, Hartmann has taken a path that has led him to a questionable end.

Hartmann's most significant contribution to the field of psychoanalysis is his essay *Ego Psychology and the Problem of Adaptation,* which was first presented in 1937 before the Vienna Psychoanalytic Society and then published in German in 1938 in the *Internationale Zeitschrift für Psychoanalyse* and *Imago.* This essay was published in an English translation by David Rapaport in 1958[10] to inaugurate the Monograph Series of the *Journal of the American Psychoanalytic Association.* Hartmann's first essay is best regarded as a prolegomenon to his later papers which, found in his collection, *Essays on Ego Psychology,*[11] expound more fully issues and conceptualizations that appear in their "unworked out" form in *Ego Psychology and the Problem of Adaptation.* The latter title encapsulates the major foci of his work: the ego and the process of adaptation. Given that the essay has been introduced as a prolegomenon, it nevertheless reads as a first and conceptually unclarified attempt to shift the entire framework of Freudian psychoanalysis sideways.

The Ego and the Problem of Adaptation

At the outset of his essay, Hartmann claims that psychoanalysis has moved from its initial study of pathology and its concentration on the id and the instinctual drives toward a *"general* theory of mental life."[12] Yet Freud was adamant that "Psycho-analysis has never claimed to provide a complete theory of human mentality in general"[13] but rather that "the theory of the neuroses is psycho-analysis itself".[14] We will see the result of this shift in connection with Hartmann's assumption concerning the subject in psychoanalysis. Given his initial thrust toward a general theory of mental life, it is not surprising that the ego forms a key focus of attention for Hartmann in his theoretical elaborations. The ego, for him, provides the basis of a psychological approach in line with an understanding of our everyday life rather than pathological or neurotic existence.

Because of this focus Hartmann proposes that the ego grows not only in conflict but that there are other roots as well, referred to when developed as the "conflict-free ego sphere." Having acknowledged Anna Freud's work on the ego and its defense functions, he points out that it is necessary to study other ego functions and other aspects of ego activity. These refer to such functions and activities as perception, intention, object comprehension, thinking, language, recall phenomena, productivity, maturation and learning processes implicit in motor development, grasping, crawling, and walking. Hence he proposes that "we adopt the provisional term *conflict-free ego sphere* for that ensemble of functions which at any time exert their effects outside the region of mental conflicts."[15] Hartmann's ego shifts the emphasis of the Freudian ego from the slave of three masters toward the ego understood as controlling agency within the terms of the everyday world. It is this ego as agent that provides the cornerstone of Hartmann's theory. While he accepts the conflicted aspects of the ego, he underscores the nonconflictual aspects and so deals at a theoretical level with the ego understood in what might be called commonsense experience. This he describes by drawing on the analogy of the description of a country. He explains that a country includes, besides its wars with neighboring territories, its boundaries and the peacetime traffic across the borders. He goes on to add that "the borderland forms an essential part of what we call, in our more usual analogy, the "central region" of the personality."[16]

Following Freud, Hartmann attributes agency to the ego or, when arguing by analogy, he imputes agency within the terms of the analogy used. For example, when employing the analogy of the function of institutions within a state he argues: ". . . A state may also be regarded as a system of institutions, which function through legislation, jurisdiction, etc. . . . Obviously, there are systematic relationships between these various points of view, and, returning to our psychological point of departure, these relationships will interest us the most".[17] The ego, like an institution, is empowered with its own controlling agency, but there is no attempt to deal with the link between agent ego and the subject in psychoanalysis. When describing the idea of ego strength, Hartmann calls on the analogy of the army to which he once again imputes the needed concept of agency. Like Freud before him, he is led to argue by analogy to deal with a concept that has not been developed adequately at a theoretical level. He writes: "The effectiveness of the armies defending the borders also depends on the support they get or do not get from the rear."[18] This means, in effect, that, true to Freud, Hartmann implicitly divides the concept of agency and the concept of the subject in psychoanalysis. The concept of agency is imputed to the psychic apparatus with all its embedded theoretical inconsistencies and contradictions. However, whereas Freud moves away from the theorization of willpower, Hartmann is interested in this concept in its own right. Hartmann is somewhat akin to Rank in the sense that the former imputes agency to the ego and thereby implicitly assumes that the subject is the subject who has the capacity to will and so determine his or her behavior. This subject is the subject in Rank's theory.

Will and the Subject

In a chapter entitled "Some Integrative Functions of the Ego" Hartmann makes a clear, though undeveloped, statement about the place of will-power in his theory. Following his observation that psychoanalysis "has lost sight of the regulation by the will,"[19] he surmises that "the psychology of will-processes is destined to play a role in the psychoanalytic ego psychology of the future."[20] What this means in effect is that Hartmann acknowledges that his ego psychology is one that embraces the notion of the efficacy of human willpower and that, to incorporate this notion, theoretical formulation is necessitated. Hartmann fails to do more than acknowledge the concept.

It could be argued that Hartmann's closest attempt to theorize on the concept of willpower is in his 1947 paper "On Rational and Irrational Action." In this paper, though not mentioning will as such, he attempts to link the structural apparatus to a theory of action. Given his emphasis on the centrality of the ego it is not surprising that he holds that "normal action in all of its varieties, even instinctual or emotional action, is formed by the ego."[21] Its link with the other institutions is understood as secondary in that action itself is named an ego function: "While the formation of action is normally accomplished by the ego, other of its characteristics may derive from the id or the super-ego."[22]

The importance of action—and one can assume willpower in acting—is best summed up in Hartmann's application of Freud's famous dictum "Where id was, there ego shall be":

> It certainly does not mean that the rational functions, or the ego interests, and so forth, could or should ever totally replace the functions of the other systems. He thought mainly of guidance by the ego, of supremacy of its organizing function, as I have described it.[23]

Undoubtedly, Hartmann's ego is the central agency in human behavior—an agency that is affected by, but in control of, the other psychic institutions. It is not until his 1950 paper "Comments on the Psychoanalytic Theory of the Ego" that Hartmann attempts to provide a much-needed clarification of his definition of the ego:

> The term "ego" is often used in a highly ambiguous way, even amongst analysts. To define it negatively in three respects, as against other ego

concepts: "ego," in analysis, is not synonymous with "personality" or with "individual"; it does not coincide with the "subject' as opposed to the "object" of experience; and it is by no means only the "awareness" or the "feelings" of one's own self. In analysis, the ego is a concept of quite a different order. It is a substructure of personality and is defined by its functions.[24]

In a very lengthy list of ego functions presented by Hartmann it is abundantly clear that his ego is the seat of human agency, although no attempt is made in his paper to theorize at the level of the analytic subject —it is as if definition from the negative absolves him of this responsibility. Is the ego conscious or unconscious or both? If it does not coincide with the subject as opposed to the object of experience, how does Hartmann understand the subject of psychological experience? If the ego is a different order, what order is this and how is it to be conceptualized? We are left at a loss in regard to these fundamental theoretical questions.

Because Hartmann claims the autonomy of the ego and maintains that will processes are important for psychoanalytic theory, we need to query the nature of the assumptions that he makes concerning the subject in psychoanalysis. We can already see that Hartmann's subject is one who wills and wishes within the context of the everyday world and that the assumptions he makes relate to a subject conceptualized within the terms of common sense. We will now see that the assumptions Hartmann does make are a direct consequence of his emphasis on adaptation and of his underpinning interest in the field of sociology.

Adaptation

The key concept, adaptation, is never very clearly spelled out in the first essay. It is certainly not restricted to a cultural sense but is presented as an ongoing process with roots in a biological structure and as a means of achieving a balance between intrasystemic and intersystemic tensions. Nevertheless Hartmann does tend to promote the idea of adapting to society's demands. This tendency can be accounted for in the light of his interest in sociology—a point to be discussed more fully in regard to his paper on the concepts of health, psychoanalysis, and sociology. In *Ego Psychology and the Problem of Adaptation* Hartmann does little more than introduce his pivotal points, with the result that it is difficult to pin down exactly what he does mean by adaptation. Although it is probably best to take it more as an emphasis or the thrust of his later theorization, he does state that the conflict-free ego sphere leads to functions "related to the tasks of reality mastering—that is, *adaptation*".[25] He goes even further in terms of his commitment to the individual's need to adapt to society when he writes: "Thus the crucial adaptation man has to make is to the social structure, and his collaboration in building it."[26]

The functions of the ego, from Hartmann's point of view, go hand in hand with or even serve this process of adaptation to the social structure. One of the most important functions that he elaborates on is the synthetic function, the organizing functions of the ego. Whereas Anna Freud defined the ego's mechanisms in terms of defense, Hartmann defines them in terms of adaptation—for example, as regulative, synthetic, or integrative functions. As far as the ego defenses are concerned, Hartmann sees inhibition as an important aspect of fitting into the social structure and claims that "defense processes may *simultaneously* serve both the control of instinctual drive and adaptation to the external world."[27] The reality principle itself is understood to imply the function of anticipating the future—a capacity of much value for the purposes of adaptation.

"Reality"

The role of the ego in regard to the reality and pleasure principles is of particular importance to the argument of this book concerning assumptions made about the subject in psychoanalysis. As with most of Hartmann's concepts, the reality principle is understood within the context of its place in the process of the ego's work of adaptation. In his 1956 paper "Notes on the Reality Principle" he defines the reality principle as "a group of ego functions," pointing out that it is to be noted that the term is used in two senses within the literature. First, it is used to indicate "a tendency to take into account in an adaptive way—in perception, thinking, and action—whatever we consider the "real" features of an object or a situation"; and second, it "represents a tendency to wrest our activities from the immediate need for discharge inherent in the pleasure principle."[28] Hartmann argues that the reality principle is not simply an opponent to the pleasure principle. It is more a principle that takes much into account and allows that amount of pleasure which is "reality syntonic." In other words, the reality principle itself allows for pleasure—it organizes delayed gratification. In addition, functions that constitute the reality principle can be pleasurable in themselves. The emphasis, then, is upon secondary processes because Hartmann argues that the ego has the possibility of pleasure in that it can, and at times does, work in the same direction as the pleasure principle. This is not only in terms of achieving instinctual satisfaction but is also associated with pleasurable feelings connected with sublimation. He assumes that dispositions for future ego functions, whose growth will later influence the pleasure and reality principles, exist at birth if not before.

The reality principle, for Hartmann, includes knowledge of reality and acting in regard to it. In developmental terms, after the development of ego functions and the constitution of constant objects and after the learned demarcation of a "self"—an undefined term—the child learns his or her approach to reality in relation to the adults's approach to it. Hartmann talks of "the taking over by the individual of the picture of reality accepted and taught by the love objects. . . . in a broader sense, of the picture commonly accepted in the culture to which he belongs".[29] This taking over also includes notions in regard to the child's inner world. The child's image of self and its evaluation, data organized and integrated by the ego, are, according to Hartmann, influenced by the child's role model and prohibiting agents. From this ego psychology perspective, the child "adjusts to a world which is not only to a considerable extent man-made, but also man-thought."[30]

When attempting to specify what constitutes reality, Hartmann, like Freud before him, veers away from philosophical theorization. However, whereas Freud looked to scientific criteria, Hartmann argues for the importance of the role of intersubjectivity in scientific validation. His reality is defined in terms of conventional thought: "But 'conventional' or 'socialized knowledge' of reality means, in contradistinction to scientific knowledge, often not so much what allows intersubjective validation, but rather what is intersubjectively accepted, to a considerable extent without validation, or attempt at validation".[31] What Hartmann has begun to venture upon is what has been taken up in great detail by the sociologists A. Schutz[32] and T. Luckmann.[33] Their work spells out much that is mentioned and alluded to in Hartmann's description of the notion of reality for ego psychology. Because the reality principle is a "group of ego functions" it is clear that Hartmann's theoretical thrust ventures very closely toward the endeavor of sociology. I will turn to this point here as Hartmann's leanings have a major influence on his implicit assumptions relating to the subject in psychoanalysis.

Psychoanalysis, Health, and Sociology

In the opening paragraph of his famous prolegomenon Hartmann refers to the problem of defining the term "reality syntonic." He then proceeds to introduce his thesis that "psychoanalysis alone cannot solve the problem of adaptation."[34] It is, he argues, a subject of research for biology and also sociology. Nonetheless, psychoanalysis, understood as ego psychology, has some considerable contribution to make because, in his terms, it has investigated the appropriate areas of inquiry:

> The increase of our interest in the problems of adaptation is due mainly to those developments in psychoanalysis which focused our attention on ego functions, but it was also fostered by our increased interest in the total personality, as well as by the concern over certain theoretical formulations about mental health, which use "adjustment to reality" as a criterion.[35]

Hartmann's emphasis, already mentioned, upon the concepts of health and adaptation to reality led him to consider his theoretical claims within the terms of the world of everyday life rather than within the terms of Freudian psychoanalysis—that is, within the terms of the field of the unconscious. In 1939 he published a paper in the *International Journal of Psycho-Analysis* entitled "Psychoanalysis and the Concept of Health." This paper provides the first in his 1964[36] collection and is followed by his 1944 paper "Psychoanalysis and Sociology."[37] These papers elaborate his attention to the concept of health and his interest in the field of sociology. They delineate the conceptual arena from which his major theoretical propositions take their initial direction. Because of a change in focus from the neuroses to the total healthy personality, Hartmann tries to talk of health within psychoanalytic terms. This attempt does little more than throw into relief the impossibility of such a refocus if one wants to remain within the field of Freudian psychoanalysis. Hartmann's conflict-free or autonomous ego is an aspect of the conventional knowledge which is his own notion of reality. It is an aspect of that shared knowledge that Schutz and Luckmann have described so well. Such knowledge pertains to the realm of phenomenological inquiry. Consequently, it is not the domain of psychoanalysis—the arena of the unconscious—but the domain of sociology, philosophy, and commonsense psychology.[38] In other words, Hartmann's leaning toward the concept of health has tipped him into the everyday social and culturally determined life world. Consequently, his theory is underpinned with assumptions that pertain to social existence rather than with assumptions that pertain to the discovery of the Freudian unconscious and consequently the subject in psychoanalysis, specifically the subject who speaks to the analyst. We are reminded here of Rank's theoretical shift out of psychoanalysis into the everyday world.

When explaining that health in the psychoanalytic sense has to mean more than simply freedom from symptoms, Hartmann points to the danger that any concept of health may be too much influenced by moral preoccupations and other subjective aspirations. He then argues that the definition needs to be along empirical lines, that is, "to examine from the point of view of their structure and development the personalities of those who are actually considered healthy instead of allowing our theoretical speculations to dictate to us what we "ought" to regard as healthy".[39] Yet the criteria for regarding someone as healthy are not defined. It is not surprising, therefore, that this paper contains a circular argument and thus toward the end Hartmann can say little more than he could at the outset:

> It is obvious that what we designate as health or illness is intimately bound up with the individual's adaptation to reality (or in the terms of an oft-repeated formula, with his sense of self-preservation).[40]

If one assumes, as does Hartmann, that the concept of the healthy personality is a focus for psychoanalysis, then, by implication, one is taking a culturally determined viewpoint; and this must be dealt with on a theoretical level. To begin an inquiry with a discussion of the concept of health is to set oneself in the direction of the world of commonsense reality, which is not the field of psychoanalysis. This is precisely what Hartmann has done and in the process lost his way. No matter how hard he tries, he finds himself in a cul-de-sac in that he wants to theorize psychoanalytically while moving into a sociological framework.

In *Ego Psychology and the Problem of Adaptation* and the later paper, "Psychoanalysis and Sociology," Hartmann makes it clear that he is very much interested in the field of sociology. In the former work he even goes so far as to write: "We hold that psychoanalysis is one of the basic sciences of sociology."[41] He argues that in sociology man is held as an achiever—that sociology studies mainly what the mental apparatus achieves and only indirectly how it masters its difficulties. We have already seen how sociological Hartmann's approach is at base given his autonomous, synthesizing, adjustment-oriented ego sphere. His hope as expressed in the prolegomenon, illustrates the direction that he was quite purposefully pursuing and one that underpins the direction of his entire endeavor:

> We hope that the study of the conflict-free ego sphere and of its functions —and the further exploration of the problem of adaptation—will open up the no-man's land between sociology and psychoanalysis.[42]

Because this no-man's land is best understood as a hybrid of psychoanalytic terms and sociological concerns, it is my contention that such a ground can produce little more than an aberration where the subject in psychoanalysis is the issue at stake.

If one plans to move out of the field of psychoanalysis one would want to be clear as to the parameters of the discipline before attempting to make the journey. Unlike in the argument concerning the concept of health where Hartmann does not delineate his field of operation, he attempts to address the problem of clarification in his 1944 paper "Psychoanalysis and Sociology": "We may ask: in what form does the relation of an individual to his fellow man and to Society come within the sphere of psycho-analysis?"[43] As he lists the ways in which this is so, Hartmann finds himself in the difficult position of acknowledging that many issues are of common interest to biology, sociology, and psychoanalysis. Although he notes the particular interest of psychoanalysis in the id, ego, and super-ego, the entire paper is beset and confounded by the nature of the argument which directs it. Hartmann's main concern here is to argue a case for the importance of psychoanalytic findings *for* sociology. Having described the social concerns of psychoanalysis, Hartmann is able to state: "We are now at a point where one can consider the research."[44] He proceeds, then, to enumerate the ways in which psychoanalytic knowledge can contribute to the social sciences. Because Hartmann has asked how psychoanalysis can contribute to sociology, he unwittingly places himself within a sociological framework to enable himself to answer the question. The really important question for psychoanalytic theory building is: What can sociology contribute to psychoanalysis? This question is

asked from within the frame of reference of psychoanalysis and, by implication, designates where the questioner stands.

Since Hartmann implicitly stands within the field of sociology, little
wonder that his ego bears the mark of so much that we take for granted
as pertaining to the subject in the world of everyday life. Little wonder,
too, that Hartmann had no need to review the assumptions underpinning
Freud's notion of the psychic apparatus. Due to his question, *Hartmann
has placed the psychic apparatus upon the theoretical assumption of the subject
in sociology.*

Conclusion

The importance of Anna Freud's work within the present context lies in
her approach to the ego and its mechanisms of defense. Irrespective of the
notable point that she fails to question the assumptions that she makes in
regard to the psychic apparatus, she did set a direction for psychoanalytic
theory construction. Given her unquestioning acceptance of the value of
Freud's second topography, she led the way for those who perceive the
ego as central and as that aspect of the psychic apparatus most worthy of
further theorization. Hartmann, likewise, took the second topography as
his theoretical framework and in a similar manner inherits the problem of
an implicit division between agency and subject. He, too, fails to recognize the nature of the assumptions that he makes and, consequently, given
his leaning toward adaptation, finds himself within a psycho-sociological
framework. His assumed subject is the subject of the everyday, commonsense world.

That Hartmann can venture to work with such an assumption is a
direct consequence of the division between the concepts of agency and
subject in Freud's theory. Because neither concept was adequately handled
at a theoretical level by Freud, later "Freudian theorists" were left free to
handle these concepts according to their own individual wont. It is not
surprising, therefore, that we find the subject in psychoanalysis portrayed
in varying ways within the literature.

This problem can be seen again in the work of Melanie Klein who, like
Hartmann, adopted Freud's topography. Whereas Hartmann's theory is
based on the assumption of the subject in the everyday world, we will

now see that Klein's theory is based on the assumption of the innately moral subject.

Melanie Klein

The work of Melanie Klein is influenced by both the first and second Freudian topographies. As early as 1914, a time when she read Freud's 1910 work on dreams *(Über den Traum)*,[45] she entered analysis with Ferenczi and, in a letter dated 14 December 1920, she mentions that she had not yet received her ordered copies of *On the Psychopathology of Everyday Life* or the latest editions of *The Interpretation of Dreams* and *Three Essays on the Theory of Sexuality*.[46] Clearly, Klein immersed herself in Freud's works, and her own early papers provide evidence of her Freudian heritage, particularly the influence of Freud's third schema (see ch. 3). Her later papers bear the influence of the fourth schema. In addition, these post *Ego and Id* works present a specifically Kleinian, as distinct from Freudian, theory of the unconscious processes and human development. Klein's work is rooted in the work of Freud, and integral to her presentations are his structural schemas of the psychic apparatus and much of his psychoanalytic terminology. For this reason her theory is embedded with the conceptual inconsistencies and contradictory assumptions that have been delineated in preceeding chapters.

Like Freud before her, Klein generally imputes agency to the psychic apparatus and consequently works with the theoretical assumption of a division between the concept of agency and the concept of the subject in psychoanalysis. In the discussion to follow we will see that it is a consequence of Freud's concept division and failure to theorize at the level of the subject in psychoanalysis that has allowed Klein to develop her own theory on the basis of a very particular notion of the subject. We will trace Klein's use of the concepts of good and bad within her theory construction. It is via this route that we will be able to gain a picture of the nature of the assumptions that she makes concerning the subject in psychoanalysis.

Inherited Problems

The first two papers that were delivered by Klein, "The Development of a Child" in 1919 to the Hungarian Society and "The Child's Resistance to Enlightenment" in 1921 to the Berlin Society, together comprise the paper now entitled "The Development of a Child." [47] In this and other early papers, Klein reports on the educational value of knowledge obtained by psychoanalysis. At this stage of her career it is clear that Klein places her work within a thoroughly Freudian perspective as evidenced by her adherence to Freud's first topography. At this time, too, Klein's work is greatly concerned with the Freudian concept of repression, which she takes to be an "innate tendency" [48] and in particular with its effects on the child's intellectual development. Within the context of her interest in the development of the child Klein contends that freedom of sexual thought is essential to the child if the individual is to achieve what she terms health, mental balance, or favorable development of character:

> We shall let the child acquire as much sexual information as the growth of its desire for knowledge requires, thus depriving sexuality at once of its mystery and of a great part of its danger. This ensures that wishes, thoughts and feelings shall not—as happened to us—be partly repressed and partly, in so far as repression fails, endured under the burden of false shame and nervous suffering, moreover, we are laying the foundations for health, mental balance and the favourable development of character. [49]

Throughout this paper and most of her early work Klein demonstrates her conviction of unconscious determination in everyday life, particularly in the school activities and play of children. For example, in her 1923 paper "The Role of the School in the Libidinal Development of the Child" she writes: "It can be repeatedly demonstrated in analyses of children that behind drawing, painting, and photography there lies a much deeper unconscious activity: it is the procreation and production in the unconscious of the object presented." [50] In the same year her paper "Early Analysis" [51] places a similar stress on the effect of repression on libidinal ideas. In addition, her own particular focus on the role of anxiety in neurosis is brought to the fore as is her suggestion that the Oedipus complex occurs at an earlier time in the child's life than Freud had stated.

Klein employs the concept of the ego in a Freudian sense in this paper. Consequently she unthinkingly takes the problem of agency into her own theorization from the start. This is exemplified in her description of the activity of the ego and repression. Klein moves conceptually from ego to subject to instinctual energy without concern as to who is the agent of action. Nor is she concerned as to how the subject is linked to the concepts of repressive forces, libidinal energies, and the self-preservative instincts that she so glibly employs in her argument:

> At the outset, then, the first reaction of the ego to the danger of a damming-up of the libido would be anxiety: "the signal for flight" . . . Another defensive measure would be submission by restriction of the libidinal tendencies, that is to say, inhibition; but this would only become possible if the subject succeeded in diverting libido on to the activities of the self-preservative instincts and thus bringing to an issue on the field of the ego-tendencies the conflict between instinctual energy and repression.[52]

This slipping and sliding of concept use is to be found throughout Klein's publications. Even though she adopts Freud's second topography and in the process of her theorizing differs from him in terms of the structural development of the psychic apparatus, she never resolves these conceptual inconsistencies. Klein's ego exists from the beginning of life, whereas it is gradually developed within Freud's theory; and her super-ego development is dated well before Freud's notions of it as heir to the Oedipus complex. Yet, although Klein postulates these differences from Freud, she never questions the nature of the assumptions that she makes about agency—and only once does she refer to the problem of the conceptualization of the notion of the subject as distinct from the psychic apparatus. This, however, was not until as late as 1959. Before then, Klein used her terms interchangeably. In 1946, for example, in "Notes on Some Schizoid Mechanisms," Klein shifts from the subject to self to ego quite inadvertently:

> By introjecting and re-introjecting the forcefully entered object, the subject's feelings of inner persecution are strongly reinforced; all the more since the re-introjected object is felt to contain the dangerous aspects of the self. The accumulation of anxieties of this nature, in which the ego is, as it were, caught between a variety of external and internal persecution-situations, is a basic element in paranoia.[53]

The same type of conceptual confusion is to be found in her 1958 presentation "On the Development of Mental Functioning" as is found in her earlier presentations. The ego, super-ego, and child are all imputed with agency and simultaneously "the child" is said to control its ego. She writes:

> But what I wish to draw attention to here, in addition to this fact, is the connection, which is observable over and over again in analysis, between a diminution of anxiety on the part of the ego in respect of the super-ego and an increased capacity in the child to become acquainted with its own intrapsychic processes and to control them more efficiently through its ego.[54]

In what sense can a child control its intrapsychic processes through its ego? What is the relationship between the concept of the child and the concept of the ego? Interestingly, a year later in her 1959 paper "Our Adult World and Its Roots in Infancy" Klein does address this issue with some directness. Having used terms haphazardly since the early twenties, she eventually recognizes that there is a need for conceptual clarification; yet the way in which she deals with the problem is not to deal with it at all. Hartmann escaped the problem with his definition by the negative; Klein escapes the problem by imagining that to raise the issue is to deal with it. One short paragraph composed of nondiscussed Freudian concepts seems to suffice:

> Before continuing my description of the child's development, I feel that I should briefly define from the psycho-analytic point of view the terms *self* and *ego*. The ego, according to Freud, is the organized part of the self, constantly influenced by instinctual impulses but keeping them under control by repression; furthermore it directs all activities and establishes and maintains the relation to the external world. The self is used to cover the whole of the personality, which includes not only the ego but the instinctual life which Freud called the id.[55]

How self and ego are linked at a theoretical level remains undisclosed; all we know is that *self* is a comprehensive term, whereas *ego* is a part of that term. What is meant by "personality" is unclear, and interestingly Klein fails to state where the super-ego fits into this definition.

Like Anna Freud and Hartmann, Klein carries into her work those problems that are the legacy of those who employ Freud's schemas of the mind without taking into account the nature of the assumptions made. Overall Klein, following Freud, constantly imputes agency to the psychic apparatus. This is well illustrated in the instance of the description of the case of Erna's play: "The hard-pressed ego tried to influence or deceive the super-ego, in order to prevent its overpowering the id, as it threatened to do. The ego tried to enlist the highly sadistic id in the service of the super-ego and to make the two combine in the fight with a common enemy."[56] After many years of trying to work the life and death instincts integrally into her theoretical formulations, Klein explains in 1958 that, whereas Freud "never fully worked out his discovery of the two instincts and seemed reluctant to extend it to the whole of mental functioning,"[57] it was her intention to do so. This means that for her "the dynamics of the mind are the result of the working of the life and death instincts"[58] and thus could be said to be her conceptualization of the notion of agency.

Klein writes, for example, that whereas Freud stated that the ego enriches itself from the id, she holds that "the ego is called into operation and developed by the life instinct."[59] The super-ego, on the other hand, in her final theorization, is the result of the ego projecting a portion of the death instinct into a part of itself that it has split off. "Accompanying this deflection of a portion of the death instinct", she states, "is a deflection of that portion of the life instinct which is fused with it."[60] The id, however, she conceptualizes in terms of being "identical with the two instincts."[61] Thus, for Klein, although agency is imputed to the psychic apparatus it is more and more linked with the notion of the life and death instincts as she attempts to conceptualize the ego, id, and super-ego in terms of these. Nevertheless, the overriding problem still remains: How is the psychic apparatus, even if it is driven by the life and death instincts, linked at a theoretical level with the subject? Furthermore, who for Klein is the subject in psychoanalysis?

The Concepts of Good and Bad and the Subject in Psychoanalysis

We have seen that Klein carried the division of the concept of agency and subject into her theoretical postulations as a direct outcome of her use of Freud's terminology and in particular of her use of his second topography. Although the influence of Freud, Ferenczi, and Abraham is evident and acknowledged by Klein, what might be considered particularly Kleinian is her emphasis upon the notion of the good and bad object within her theoretical contributions. The introduction of this moral terminology is to be found very early in her work and not only remains throughout her papers but also becomes increasingly important and central to her theorization.

In her early papers Klein was particularly interested in what she described as an early phase of sadism. She contends that this phase, ushered in by the child's oral-sadistic desire to devour the mother's breast and passing away with the anal stage, forms the introduction to the Oedipus complex. By 1928 Klein could postulate that Oedipal tendencies make their appearance at the end of the first and the beginning of the second year of life and that the super-ego is built up of identifications dating from very different periods in the mental life. "The identifications," she states, "are surprisingly contradictory in nature, excessive goodness and excessive severity existing side by side."[62] Whereas Freud stressed the mechanism of repression, as did Klein in her very early work, she now stresses the mechanisms of splitting, projection, and introjection—the infant splits imagos and objects into extreme types, projecting and introjecting them in an attempt to deal with the anxiety that is a product of its early sadism. The notion of extreme types is mentioned, for example, in her 1929 paper "Personification in the Play of Children" in terms of "the intensity of the need for the kindly figures in opposition to the menacing,"[63] but it is in 1931 when this idea of opposites is transformed into the good/bad conceptualization. Here, when discussing her theory of intellectual inhibition, Klein describes John's activity in the following symbolic terms:

> When John tidied his drawer he was tidying his own body and separating his own possessions from the things he had stolen out of his mother's body, as well as separating "bad" faeces from "good" faeces, and 'bad' objects from 'good' ones. In doing this John likened the broken, damaged and dirty things to the "bad" object, "bad" faeces and "bad" children, in accordance with the workings of the unconscious, where the damaged object becomes a "bad" and dangerous one.[64]

What is important to note here is the interchange between "bad" and "broken, damaged and dirty." No synonym for "good" is provided at this stage, but we will see how "good" and "bad" are used interchangeably with nonmoralistic concepts. Inverted commas are used in this paper and in many others but there is no consistency about this throughout her work. Perhaps most important of all is that Klein never really defines what she means by "good" and "bad"—she simply inserts the terms into her text without providing any rationale as to the need for their introduction.

It is as if "good" and "bad" are summary terms for all the other words and phrases that she uses in place of them.

By 1932, when Klein published her now-famous book *The Psycho-Analysis of Children*,[65] the good/bad terminology had become an accepted component of her general vocabulary. Yet it does seem that is was while compiling this book that Klein worked them permanently into her theory and by implication had begun to think of the subject as an innately moral being who could, from very early infancy, impute a moral order to its world.

Notably in chapter 8 there is no mention of the moral good/bad terms. Instead Klein writes in psychological terms when describing the split between objects and the distinction between inner and outer worlds with which, she argues, the child has to contend:

> In the early stages, the projection of his terrifying imagos into the external world turns that world into a place of danger and his objects into enemies, while the simultaneous introjections of real objects which are in fact well-disposed to him, works in the opposite direction and lessens the force of his fear of the terrifying imagos.[66]

Yet, in chapter 9 she writes in distinctly moral terms describing the small child's relationship to unreal imagos, which she says "are experienced both as excessively good and as excessively bad."[67] She goes on later to mention what is to become a key idea in her theory—"This process of relating to objects is brought about by a splitting up of the mother-imago into a good and a bad one."[68]

The insertion of a moral order into her theory is particularly clear by the time Klein is ready to theorize about the sexual development of the girl and of the boy. "Good" and "bad" are central terms and are well and truly embedded within her thought at this stage. Yet, at the same time, Klein utilizes her nonmoralistic vocabulary almost alternatively. She explains that it is of decisive importance for the formation of the super-ego and the development of sexual life in the girl "whether the prevailing fantasies are those of a "good" or a "bad" penis."[69] Klein continues: "In favorable circumstances the girl believes in the existence of a dangerous, introjected penis, as well as a beneficial helpful one".[70] "Good" seems synonymous with beneficial and helpful and "bad" synonymous with dangerous. Klein postulates that in normal sexual development the girl fears the introjected "bad" penis, and it is this fear that acts as an incentive to her continually introjecting a "good" one in coitus. In other words, the notion of good/bad introjections have long-term consequences for the girl's later choice of love object or partner and have an effect on her desire for a child. Klein explains that the girl's sexual development starts with the introjection of her mother's breast followed by a desire for the father's penis. "Good" and "bad" are central to her formulation of the transposition of the girl's desire:

> The first objects that she introjects are her "good" mother and her "bad" one, as represented by the breast. Her desire to suck or devour the penis is directly derived from her desire to do the same to her mother's breast so that the frustration she suffers from the breast prepares the way for the feelings which her renewed frustration in regard to the penis arouses.[71]

An important footnote[72] here states that in chapter 8 Klein showed how the "good" breast becomes turned into a "bad" one in consequence of the child's imaginary attacks upon it, yet nowhere in chapter 8 are the terms *good* and *bad* employed. This footnote suggests that at this point Klein reached what for her was conceptual clarification by way of the good/bad moral framework which had become increasingly important to her formulation. Here, it seems, she retrospectively brings to bear upon her earlier psychological explanations the moral framework that is crucial to the nature of the assumptions she makes about the subject in her work.

Good/bad also fit into Klein's growing interest in the idea of restitution. She contends that in the face of the infant's sadistic fantasies the child attempts to restore what has been damaged, spoiled, and broken. Thus she argues that in dividing its mother into a "good" mother and a "bad" one, and its father into a "good" and a "bad" one, the child "attaches the hatred it feels for its object to the 'bad' one or turns away from it, while it directs its restorative trends to its 'good' mother and 'good' father and, in fantasy, makes good towards them the damage it has done its parent-imagos in its sadistic fantasies."[73] Just as in the case of the girl's sexual development, good and bad are crucial concepts in Klein's discussion of the boy's sexual development. Again, as in the instance of the girl, I do not intend to go into details. However, suffice it to note as an example that Klein proposes that "the foundation of a successful male development is the supremacy of the 'good' mother-imago which assists the boy to overcome his sadism and works against all his fears."[74] The idea of restitution is also involved in Klein's theory of the boy's sexual development. She holds that at a very early stage the boy believes in the sadistic qualities of his father's penis by projecting his own sadism onto it. In fantasy the child transforms this penis into "a 'good' organ with healing powers" through his restitutive fantasies and sense of guilt.[75]

It appears that by the time Klein had written her 1932 work, the concepts of good and bad were what might be considered taken-for-granteds within her theoretical terminology. Certainly by this time embedded in her work is the assumption that the subject has an innate capacity to attribute a moral order to inner and outer worlds. Yet, it is especially significant that in 1935 when she launched into her construction of a new theoretical scaffolding with the now-classic paper "A Contribution to the Psychogenesis of Manic-Depressive States", her opening paragraph addressed the issue of the theoretical rationale behind her notion of good and bad. Klein restated her interest in the phase of sadism through which children pass during the first year of life, then proceeded to give an account of mechanisms involved in the earliest stage of the infant's psychological development:

> The development of the infant is governed by the mechanisms of introjection and projection. From the beginning the ego introjects objects "good" and "bad," for both of which the mother's breast is the prototype—for good objects when the child obtains it, for bad ones when it fails him. But it is because the baby projects its own aggression on to these objects that it feels them to be "bad" and not only in that they frustrate its desires . . . These imagos, which are a phantastically distorted picture of the real objects upon which they are based, become installed not only in the outside world but, by the process of incorporation, also within the ego.[76]

What is noteworthy here is that aggression is posited as synonymous with "bad" in addition to the link between felt frustration and the concept of "bad." Why is aggression necessarily bad? Could not aggression be aggression pure and simple without any overlay of a moral code? Klein does not argue a case here, she merely continues to stipulate her position. Furthermore, we are left without any mention of why the infant experiences the mother's breast as necessarily "good" other than that satisfaction is associated with "good" just as frustration is said to be associated with "bad." How can the infant, as yet still in the phase of early sadism, project "goodness" onto the breast? The projection of goodness from a sadistic phase would seem to be logically inconsistent, yet it is a Kleinian postulate at this point in her theory construction. Some further statement about the "goodness" of the good breast is needed because the latter concept is vital to her theory of ego development. This is so because for Klein the ego gradually identifies with "good" objects and the fear of persecution that is initially felt by the ego is overcome with these identifications—so much so that "preservation of the good object is regarded as synonymous with the survival of the ego."[77]

In addition, the idea of goodness is crucial to Klein's theory of restitutive processes. Why does the infant feel a need to restore that which its sadistic and "bad" impulses have destroyed? An imputed moral order alone gives a rationale for this need. Without it the infant might happily accept the result of its destruction. Klein does not provide a rationale for the importance of this moral order which is central to her formulations. In her 1935 paper she simply asserts that the ego "feels impelled (and I can now add, impelled by its identification with the good object) to make restitution for all the sadistic attacks that it has launched on that object".[78]

Although we are still left without a reason for the projection of goodness during the sadistic phase or left unsure as to whether the child automatically divides the world into good/bad, introjecting goodness and projecting badness, Klein continues to rely on the moral code in her descriptions and delineations of psychopathology. For example, the melancholic is described as needing to comply with the strict demands of the "good" objects whereas the depressive is said to try to preserve the "good" internalized objects. This means that here Klein holds as central to her theoretical postulations a moral code or register that has never been adequately explained. Interestingly, this moral order is used interchangeably with what has also become important within her theory: the use of the terms *love* and *hate*.

In the 1935 paper Klein talks of the infant splitting its imagos into "loved and hated, that is to say, into good and dangerous ones."[79] This statement is not only unbalanced by the loss of the concept bad, but the moral order also seems superfluous in itself. Would not loved and hated objects be enough? It does seem that the moral register is needed to provide an implicit "cognitive motor" for her theory of restitution. In 1940 Klein was no further advanced in providing a satisfactory explanation. She continued to reassert her position concerning the importance of good and bad objects to the individual's psychic life. Here, however, objects are good and bad because the individual *feels* them to be so:

As I have often pointed out, the processes of introjection and projection from the beginning of life lead to the institution inside ourselves of loved and hated objects, who are felt to be "good" and "bad," and who are interrelated with each other and with the self: that is to say, they constitute an inner world.[80]

Then, in 1946, Klein approached the problem of good/bad again. This time there is an important difference. In her paper "Notes on Some Schizoid Mechanisms" she links good with wholeness and bad with bits and pieces. She proposes a paranoid-schizoid position as being prior in the infant's development to the depressive position that she put forward in 1935. It is within this context that Klein argues that during the oral sadistic phase the infant feels that it has taken in "the nipple and the breast *in bits*. Therefore," she argues, "in addition to the division between a good and a bad breast in the infant's fantasy, the frustrating breast— attacked in oral-sadistic fantasies—is felt to be in fragments; the gratify-ing breast, taken in under the dominance of the sucking libido, is felt to be complete."[81] It is this first internal good object that acts as a central point in the ego. So now we have a theoretical statement in which Klein introduces the idea of a link between libido and the good breast—the good breast is good because it is taken in under the dominance of libido —as well as a new association between good and wholeness and bad and bits and pieces. Even though one has to assume here that libido is in some sense good, this paper does provide theoretical elucidation concerning her theory of ego development. In addition, this paper marks yet again the nature of the assumptions that Klein makes about the subject in her theory. Because good and bad objects are pivotal to the development of the ego, to sexuality, and to interpersonal relationships, it is essential to Klein that the subject can from its earliest infancy, divide the world into good and bad. This subject is, therefore, an innately moral one.

Although by the 1950s Klein had moved from her early reliance on Freud's (and Abraham's) psychosexual developmental stages to her own formulation of the paranoid-schizoid and depressive positions, she contin-ued to work with Freud's theory of the life and death drives. Whereas in her early work she paid much attention to aggression, her theory of developmental positions allowed her to introduce the idea of love and hate more fully into her conceptualizations. As mentioned, Klein used love and hate interchangeably with good and bad, but as her work gained clarity and consistency she was able in 1952 to take into account a number of issues that troubled her theory. She still simply asserts without provi-sion of theoretical explanation that inasmuch as the breast is gratifying it "is loved and felt to be 'good'; in so far as it is a source of frustration, it is hated and felt to be 'bad' . . ."[82] However, she does now posit the idea of the good breast attaining its status via the mechanism of projection, thereby providing the balance missing in her 1935 opening paragraph:

> In addition to the experiences of gratification and frustration derived from external factors, a variety of endopsychic processes—primarily introjection and projection—contribute to the twofold relation to the first object. The infant projects his love impulses and attributes them to the gratifying (good) breast, just as he projects his destructive impulses outwards and attributes them to the frustrating (bad) breast . . . The good breast, external and internal—becomes the prototype of all helpful and gratifying objects, the bad breast the prototype of all external and internal persecuting objects.[83]

The good breast is here deemed good on account of the projection of love impulses, whereas the bad is deemed bad on account of the projection of destructive impulses. Just as Klein fails to theorize as to why satisfaction is necessarily felt to be good and frustration necessarily felt to be bad, neither does she explain why love is directed to good and destruction to bad objects. In other words, although Klein has brought what might be termed cognitive balance to her theory with her introduction of the projection of love impulses as well as destructive ones in early infancy, she never does more than impute this good/bad moral order to the infant's world. This means that her use of a moral order persists without theoretical rationalization.

Even by 1958 when, in her paper "The Development of Mental Functioning," Klein elaborates upon her interest in Freud's instinct theory and the way in which she deviates from him in its regard, she still bypasses this central theoretical problem of a moral order. By this time she had worked the instincts and their expression into her theory with sufficient clarity to be able to explain many of her earlier conceptualizations as being underpinned by "the all-pervading power of the life and death instincts."[84] In the instance of the concepts of good and bad she explains as follows:

> From the beginning of life the two instincts attach themselves to objects, first of all the mother's breast . . . According to whether destructive impulses or feelings of love predominate, the breast (for which the bottle can symbolically come to stand) is felt at times to be good, at times to be bad. The libidinal cathexis of the breast, together with gratifying experiences,

builds up in the infant's mind the primal good object, the projection on the breast of destructive impulses the primal bad object. Both these aspects are introjected and thus the life and death instincts, which had been projected, again operate within the ego.[85]

Later, within the same paper she contends:

The contrast between persecutory and idealized, between good and bad objects—being an expression of life and death instincts and forming the basis of fantasy life—is to be found in every layer of the self.[86]

Conclusion

Klein introduced the concepts of good and bad into her pre-1935 work without any theoretical justification. Not only did they remain embedded within her psychoanalytic thought but they also became more and more central to her formulations as she built a specifically Kleinian body of psychoanalytic theory. The notion of good/bad is integral to her conceptualization of the developmental positions, ego development, sexual development, and psychopathology. The idea of good and bad objects pertains to both the inner and outer world which are both components of her theory, and good and bad objects are also associated with the mechanisms of introjection and projection which claim a pivotal role in her exposition of the infant's psychic world.

Klein's theory is without two needed theoretical explanations: one in which the connection made between the child's experience of the outer world in terms of either satisfying or frustrating breast with *felt* goodness and *felt* badness is elucidated and the other in which the connection made between the expression of life and death drive and goodness and badness is elucidated. Klein provides neither of these necessary explanations and consequently leaves herself open to the accusation of the unjustified employment of moral terminology in her theory. Furthermore, it would be possible for Klein to hypothesize in terms of the infant's splitting the world into satisfying and frustrating and in terms of the infant's fantasy being an expression of the life and death drives, even if these are referred to via the concept of love and hate, without any mention of a moral order. In other words, her theory does not really need the insertion of a moral order—at least at a descriptive level. However, where a moral order does seem essential to her theory is with regard to the dynamic underlying her notion of reparative processes or restitution. Unless the infant feels bad about its sadistic attacks, there seems little need for any form of reparation to take place. Destruction could simply remain destruction and life go on. Only in the light of a felt guilt need the infant wish to restore that which has been damaged. If the infant conceptualizes in terms of good/bad, then we can assume that guilt will follow the sense of badness. In Kleinian terms, this guilt will be assuaged through restitutive processes. Because the movement from the paranoid-schizoid position through the depressive position to health is integrally bound to the idea of reparative processes, and as this is Kleinian theory par excellence, a moral order is essential to her psychoanalytic thought.

I will not venture here into the problem as to whether or not an infant can divide the world into good/bad by means of adequately developed cognitive processes within its first year. Irrespective of this issue, and it is an important one, what has become clear is that Klein imputes a moral order to the very young infant. For her, *the infant is an innately moral subject,* one who brings moral cognitive processes to bear on its earliest experiences of the world, both inner and outer. In her theory the infant does not "learn" what is said to be good or bad within a cultural context but rather innately knows of the distinction and automatically applies it to sensations and impulses alike. Without this assumption of an innate morality Klein's theory lacks the necessary motor for the reparative processes that she proposes, which are pivotal to her contribution to the field of psychoanalytic thought.

We have seen the consequences of the concept split between the notion of agency and the notion of the subject, found in Freud's theory construction, as it played out in the work of Heinz Hartmann. Hartmann based his psychoanalytic thought on the assumption of what I have described as the subject in sociology. In the work of Melanie Klein, however, a very different assumption is made—one of a moral subject because this is necessary to her theoretical exposition. That two such very different subjects can emerge within the history of psychoanalytic thought is a Freudian inheritance. This is so in so far as these two theorists, employing Freud's schema of the mind with its imputed agency, were left to base their work on the assumption of that subject that best befitted the psychoanalytic postulations they preferred.

In neither instance do we find that the assumptions made are in line with characterization of the subject of our point of departure, the *hysté-*

rique d'occasion. This subject, who spoke to Freud of her inability to do what she so much wanted to do, is distinguished by two main features: first, that she is a being who speaks and, second, that there is something beyond conscious willpower that controls her on certain occasions. The subject in psychoanalysis is, then, best conceptualized in terms of these two characteristics, speech and the unconscious. Freud's schema of the psychic apparatus is an attempt to deal with the notion of the unconscious and, so, the problem of agency. Even though I have argued that his attempt is inadequate, both Hartmann and Klein can be said to have attempted to deal with the problem of ineffective willpower by way of their use of the Freudian schema. This means that they attend to one characteristic alone: that of the concept of the unconscious. However, the assumptions made by these theorists about the subject within their theory construction in no way bear directly upon the other of those features that are held to be specific to the notion of the subject in psychoanalysis— namely, that of speech. Neither the subject in sociology nor the subject who is innately moral is necessarily characterized by the capacity to employ the spoken word. The former is characterized by his or her place in the everyday world, the latter by his or her ability to conceptualize the world in moral terms.

In the work of Jacques Lacan, however, we find the subject understood in terms of the being who speaks. For this reason his work is especially important to the argument of this book. Yet he, too, like Freud before him, separates the concept of the subject and the concept of agency. In so doing he creates a problem at a theoretical level. It is to his work that we now turn.

7

A Problem Concerning Agency
in Psychoanalysis

Jacques Lacan

Although both the figure and teaching of Jacques Lacan are controversial, there is no doubt that his contribution to the theory and practice of psychoanalysis is of paramount importance. Within the present context his work holds particular interest because of the direct attention that he pays to the problem of the subject in psychoanalysis and because of his approach to the issue of agency. Lacan places his subject within the symbolic world, the world of language. This means that his theory deals with the subject understood in terms of the subject who speaks to the analyst. However, although he emphasizes the relationship between the subject in psychoanalysis and speech—an emphasis that I deem crucial to psychoanalytic theory construction—his theory of the subject is fraught with difficulties. It is in the light of these difficulties that a number of commentators argue that, for Lacan, there are two subjects. This, of course, poses conceptual problems. More important to the present argument is the point that Lacan divides the concept of the subject and the concept of agency. Particularly interesting in his work is the way in which he imputes the concept of agency to language with the consequence that within his theory the subject is said to be constituted by the symbolic order.

As mentioned in the introduction, I will focus on the early work of Lacan. Although this is the Lacan of the English-speaking world, it is also true that in his early years Lacan was especially interested in the symbolic. In his later years he became more and more interested in the concept of the Real. This concept, taken with the Symbolic and Imaginary, form the ground of his psychoanalytic thinking. We shall briefly give some attention to the Real later in this chapter.

To begin, I will very concisely outline Lacan's theory of the subject to show his proposition of a divided subject. I will then look in detail at the nature of his assumption concerning agency by paying attention to the text that is quintessential Lacan: the "Seminar on 'The Purloined Letter.'"[1] Most importantly I want to show that, given the assumption of the agency of the signifier, there are numerous instances where Lacan's proposition concerning the subject in psychoanalysis results in a theoretical impasse. At such times Lacan imputes agency to the subject while maintaining the theoretical stance that the subject is entirely determined by the signifier—a concept crucial to his linguistic approach.

Lacan's Theory of the Subject in Psychoanalysis

Rather than propose a theory of the psychic apparatus, or simply unquestioningly adopt that devised by Freud, Lacan addresses the theory of the subject in psychoanalysis. In so doing he explores at a theoretical level what others fail to acknowledge at the level of theoretical assumptions. However, it is at the level of theoretical explanation that Lacan's conceptualizations are so difficult to handle. Lacan's theory of the subject cannot be understood in everyday terms. This is so not only because of his emphasis on structural linguistics and because of the terminology he employs—both of which are alien to everyday discourse—but also because of his polemic against the emphasis of the ego psychologists. The latter, I have argued, base their work on the assumption of the subject in sociology or the subject of the everyday world. In his theory Lacan protests against the idea that the ego is the controlling center of the individual. He offensively shatters the everyday man's illusion of wholeness and propounds the idea that the subject is subject to unconscious desire. This desire is constituted by the circuit of signifiers—that is, language—within which the subject is circumscribed. This means, in effect, that for Lacan the subject is decentered; that is, the subject lives out of a truth, a desire, unknown to any individual in everyday life.

Consequently, in Lacan's theory great emphasis is placed on the notion of subjectivity and otherness and ultimately on the agency of the signifier in the construction of the subject.

Lacan drew upon numerous disciplines in the elaboration of his theory, consequently his definitions of the subject alter according to the theoretical context within which each conceptualization is made. Nevertheless, his subject is never defined in essentialist terms, nor is it defined in empirical, psychological, or physiological terms; more often it is, as D. Funt explains, "a requirement of the discourse, the place, as it were, left vacant by the discourse."[2] The difficulty of coming to grips with Lacan's conceptualization of the subject is highlighted in *Book II* of the Seminar series in which one interlocutor, Dr. Leclaire, continually draws attention to Lacan's reticence in dealing adequately with the subject at a theoretical level. Leclaire is adamant that the subject cannot be put in brackets and is consequently accused of idolatry:

> Dr. Leclaire: I'm sorry, but I'd like to reply. If I have a tendency to idolize the subject, it's because I think it necessary—you can't do otherwise.
> Lacan: Well, then, you are a little idolator. I come down from Sinai and break the Tables of the Law.[3]

Later Leclaire continues:

> I simply have the feeling that this phenomenon of avoidance is reproduced every time we speak of the subject. Every time, it is a kind of reaction, when we speak of the subject.[4]

Lacan breaks the Tables of the Law by means of taking the *Spaltung,* or splitting, seriously—that is, by taking the split subject as the subject of his theory. For him, the subject suffers the *Spaltung* "from its subordination to the signifier,"[5] and it is the nature and consequence of this splitting that occupies much of Lacan's theorizing. I will turn now to outline briefly the gist of Lacan's approach to the subject, a theory that can to some degree be illustrated by way of his notion of the mirror stage and Schema L.

The Mirror Stage

In 1936 Lacan presented a paper "The Mirror Stage" to the International Psychoanalytic Congress in Marienbad. Although the paper was not published at the time it appears in *Écrits* (1966) as the revised version that was delivered at Zurich to the International Congress in 1949.[6] This paper employs Freud's concept of narcissism and some aspects of his formulations on ego formation. As is usual for Lacan, emphasis is placed on Freud's first topography.

According to Lacan, the mirror stage occurs between the age of six to eighteen months. At this stage the child is capable of seeing and recognizing its own image in the mirror—this is not necessarily in practical terms but refers to the image provided by the mother or caretaker. Physically speaking the child is uncoordinated at this age, but the image gives the baby a sense of unity and wholeness that it cannot itself experience. Prior to this stage, the child experiences its body in bits and pieces. This means, in effect, that at the mirror stage, an imaginary mastery is set up.

For Lacan, the ego takes its form from this image and in this way the ego is the basis of an imaginary relationship of the subject with his/her own body. Hence, in this formulation there is an alienation between the subject and the image or ego. Lacan argues that ego development, based on an imaginary relationship of a child with its own body, continues as the subject identifies with the image of the human form via other human beings:

> The *mirror stage* is a drama whose internal thrust is precipitated from insufficiency to anticipation—and which manufactures for the subject, caught up in the line of spatial identification, the succession of fantasies that extends from a fragmented body-image to a form of its totality that I shall call orthopedic—and, lastly, to the assumption of the armor of an alienating identity, which will mark with its rigid structure the subject's entire mental development.[7]

This split or alienation between the ego and the subject has broad consequences. According to Lacan, the ego is the seat of what he terms *méconnaissance,* of mis-knowledge. This is so because truth is alien to the ego, its home being with the subject. Thus Lacan claims that the ego refuses the truth of the subject—that is, refuses to acknowledge the subject's thoughts and feelings. The ego can do nothing other, however, due to its alienated and alienating position—that is, due to the split between the image or imaginary figure and the subject itself. It is for this reason that Lacan is uncompromising in his criticism of the ego theorists who follow Hartmann's theoretical position. Having criticized their position in his paper he writes:

Our experience shows us that we should start instead from the *function of
méconnaissance* that characterizes the ego in all its structures so markedly
articulated by Miss Anna Freud. For, if the *Verneinung* (denial) represents
the patent form of that function, its effects, will, for the most part, remain
latent, so long as they are not illuminated by some light reflected on to the
level of fatality, which is where the id manifests itself.[8]

Given the mirror stage and the constitution of the ego as described, it
is clear that from very early Lacan's theory of the subject incorporates the
notion of intersubjectivity. The other, be that the mother or caretaker, is
an important figure in the child's earliest identifications. Moreover, the
mother or (m)other, as a source of the child's imaginary image, is important with regard to the unconscious. At the end of the mirror stage this
image is repressed as the core of desire in the child's unconscious. This
means, therefore, that Lacan's concept of desire is one that necessarily
divides the subject. The child lives out of unconscious desire while simultaneously and necessarily being deceived by the mis-knowledge that structures the ego. Put in other words, the desire of the human being is, for
Lacan, the desire of the Other. The distinction drawn between unconscious desire and everyday conscious want is defined by Lacan in terms of
a distinction among need, demand, and desire. The distinction Lacan
describes as follows:

> Thus desire is neither the appetite for satisfaction, nor the demand for love,
> but the difference that results from the subtraction of the first from the
> second, the phenomenon of their splitting.[9]

Need, according to Lacan, is something physical; it pertains to what
might be called organic drive toward organic satisfaction. Demand, however, pertains to the notion of an appeal for love. Desire, unlike the
former concepts that belong to conscious discourse, belongs to the realm
of the unconscious. It is representational in that it refers to a referential
content of images and meaning inscribed in the place of the Other and, as
well, it is an indestructable force that is evidenced as an insatiable yearn-
ing. The latter two aspects of desire are linked at a theoretical level to the
mirror stage outlined earlier.

The issue of desire in Lacan is a complex one,[10] but it consistently
appears conceptualized in relation to the idea of lack. In the mirror stage
the child begins to repress identificatory images, and when the image of
the (m)other is repressed the child's symbolic union with the mother is
lost. It is from the source of this lack or loss that desire is born. This

initial separation from the mother is a crucial historical event in the individual's process of coming to be a human being. From this point onward, for example, the child searches ceaselessly for replacements for that which it lacks, but, for that which it can never find. A failure in separation then, has profound implications concerning the individual's desire.

In addition, at about eighteen months the child begins to speak. It is through this linguistic ability itself that the subject suffers yet another dimension of the *Spaltung*. This is so in the sense that by the use of words which symbolize the (m)other, the child accepts language as a substitute for the lost union that is so desired but that can never be achieved. When the child utters "Mummy" the verbal representation or symbolization acts as a substitute for that which the child lacks—the primary union with the mother. Yet, it is this very utterance that builds absence or lack into the structure of the subject and ensures that the speaking being will be marked by unsatisfied wanting. It is through language that the individual's endless desire is expressed and the *Spaltung* enacted.

If we accept the radical distinction between the ego and subject as proposed by Lacan we are nevertheless still left with the problem of what Lacan means by his notion of the subject in his theory. The ego is an image. That is clear, but as to how the notion of the subject is to be understood remains an area of ambiguity and indecisiveness. Leclaire's noted comment that a "phenomenon of avoidance is produced every time we speak of the subject" seems more than apt.

Sometimes Lacan speaks of "the unconscious subject,"[11] but the meaning of this terms is difficult to understand. Does Lacan imply that the subject does not know of its existence, or does this term imply that the subject is responsible for behavior that is instigated by that aspect of the individual which is to be differentiated from the ego? At other times he implies that the subject is *in* the unconscious, whereas elsewhere it seems that for Lacan the subject is understood to be subject *to* the unconscious. For example, in *Seminar II* he says, ". . . according to Freud the reality of the subject is. In the unconscious, excluded from the system of the ego, the subject speaks."[12] Here the subject is said to speak within or through the unconscious. Thus, there is a subject and an unconscious. There is no doubt that it is the subject who speaks, not the unconscious, yet it is unclear as to which is master.

Lacan even suggests a topographical idea where in the same discussion he admits to his search for the subject: "So here we are," states Lacan, "in search of the subject . . . The question is to know where it is. That it is in the unconscious at least so far as we analysts are concerned, is the point I believe I've led you to and which I am now reaching myself."[13] In *Seminar II* Lacan also talks in terms of "the subject of the unconscious." He does so when he speaks of the radical difference and dissymmetry between the ego and the subject as follows: ". . . an absolute dissymmetry between the subject of the unconscious and the organization of the ego, but also a radical difference."[14] What is implied by the phrase "the subject of the unconscious"? Does Lacan here suggest that there is a subject of the unconscious and a subject of the conscious? Discrepancies in his formulations can be evidenced yet again where Lacan speaks of the dream of Irma's injection. He states: "What is at stake in the function of the dream is beyond the *ego,* what in the subject is of the subject and not of the subject, that is the unconscious."[15] Here we are presented with the unconscious defined in terms of the subject rather than the subject referred to in relation to the unconscious. Just as Hartmann defined the self by the negative and Klein dealt with the notion of the self in one paragraph, Lacan deals with his central concept of the subject by defining it in relation to other theoretical concepts—in particular, the unconscious.

Even if we accept this style, we are nevertheless left with such shifting meanings that, at most, all we can say is, in this context the use of the term means such and such. What is meant by the split between the ego and subject is also difficult to decipher, especially in the light of what Lacan refers to as the structuration of the subject: "the ego can in no way be anything else other than an imaginary function, even if at a certain level it determines the structuration of the subject."[16] How does the ego determine the structuration of the subject? What is the nature of the link between the ego and the subject if there is, in his words, "a radical difference" between them? What is meant by the term *structuration?* Does Lacan impute agency to the ego here, or does he refer in some way to the symbolic register alone? Given that these statements are taken from the transcripts of his *Seminar* series, we can expect difficulties in understanding to ensue; but the real problem is that Lacan has never fully documented an elaboration of his theory, and in many instances all that we are left with are unspelled-out propositions to which he gives much weight and credence. It should be mentioned here, too, that Lacan's use of the term *structuration* is in no way synonymous with the use of the terms to be presented in the following chapter.

In his difficult work "The Subversion of the Subject and the Dialectic of Desire in the Freudian Unconscious," the text representing his contribution to a conference at Royaumont 1960, Lacan searches again for his subject. This time he employs a linguistic framework and poses the question with poignancy: "Once the structure of language has been recognized in the unconscious, what sort of subject can we conceive for it?"[17] This time his reply concerns the notion of the subject *of,* rather than *in,* the unconscious:

> "Who is speaking?" when it is the subject of the unconscious that is at issue. For this reply cannot come from that subject if he does not know what he is saying or even if he is speaking, as the entire experience of analysis has taught us.
> It follows that the place of the "inter-said" (inter-dit), which is the "intra-said" (intra-dit) of a between-two-subjects, is the very place in which the transparency of the classical subject is divided and passes through the effects of "fading" that specify the Freudian subject by its occultation by an even purer signifier.[18]

This answer suggests that the subject is a locus in the discourse—a locus found somewhere in the cut or split between two subjects—presumably, the subject of consciousness and the subject of the unconscious or, conceptualized alternatively, between the ego and the subject. Thus it is that Lacan can claim: "I think where I am not, therefore I am where I do not think" or, again, "I am not wherever I am the plaything of my thought; I think of what I am where I do not think to think."[19]

Lacan leaves us in uncertainty as to his stance. Perhaps these conceptual shifts are an indication of his own uncertainty if not his constantly changing theoretical speculations. If there is one point that is clear it is that for Lacan the ego is not the subject. It is to an elaboration of this point that Lacan turns when he attempts to present his theory of the subject in a schematic form.

Schema L

Schema L can be understood as Lacan's attempt to provide a two-dimensional representation of his theory of the split subject. Schema L first appears in *Seminar II,* "Play of Writings"[20] and reappears later in the transcript.[21] With it he provides a schema that illustrates different planes and processes involved in his theory of the ego and subject.

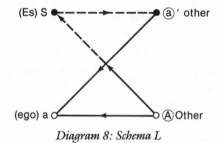

Diagram 8: Schema L

Lacan explains that S designates the subject but carefully stipulates, "the analytic subject, that is to say not the subject in its totality. . . . It is the subject, not in its totality, but in its opening up."[22] Again it is unclear as to what he means by the subject, but he continues to explain that the subject sees himself in a; that is why he has an ego. Lacan then expounds on the intersubjective nature of his formulation, an aspect noted in the constitution of the ego in the mirror stage. The ego, he says, "perceives what we call for structural reasons its fellow beings, in the form of the specular other. This form of the other has a very close relation to the ego, which can be superimposed on it, and we write it as a'."[23] Here we can see the process by which progressive identifications take place. Drawing upon Euclidean geometry Lacan represents two planes in the schema: the Imaginary (a'-a) (ego and its image or imaginary counterpart) and the Symbolic (A-S) through which the subject is alienated. In our experience of everyday life we think we live out of the imaginary, but this is no more than a function of the ego's *méconnaissance*. In analysis the analyst, working along the symbolic plane, works with the truth or, as Lacan says, with "true subjects." Schema L makes the important point of a topographical distinction between the ego and the subject. This distinction is so vital that Lacan can say:

> One trains analysts so that there are subjects in whom the ego is absent. That is the ideal of analysis, which, of course, remains virtual. There is never a subject without an ego, a fully realized subject, but that in fact is what one must aim to obtain from the subject in analysis.[24]

The ego is not considered to be the analytic subject, but rather Lacan speaks of it as if it were an attribute of the subject. Similarly, in his important work "The Function and Field of Speech and Language in Psychoanalysis," Lacan speaks of the ego and the "I," the *moi* and the *je*, but maintains the notion of *a* subject who has an ego and an "I":

> It is therefore always in the relation between the subject's ego *(moi)* and the "I" *(je)* of his discourse that you must understand the meaning of the discourse if you are to achieve the dealienation of the subject.
>
> But you cannot possibly achieve this if you cling to the idea that the ego of the subject is identical with the presence that is speaking to you.[25]

As in *Seminar II* he argues again toward the ideal of a nonalienated subject as the outcome of psychoanalysis. Here, once more, Lacan implies that there is *a* subject which has an ego and an I of discourse: "It is therefore always in the relation between the subject's ego *(moi)* and the "I" *(je)* of his discourse that you must understand the meaning of the discourse if you are to achieve the dealienation of the subject."[26]

It is one thing to argue a case for a subject and an ego. It is another to argue for a split subject and another again to argue a case for two subjects. To indicate that the subject of psychoanalysis is to be found between two subjects is yet another position. We have seen that Lacan puts forward each of these propositions, and in later work he continues to posit new conceptualizations that involve his complex approach to the subject in psychoanalysis.

Within one paper numerous definitions are to be found. For example, in "Of Structure as an Inmixing of an Otherness Prerequisite to Any Subject Whatever" he explains that "the subject is the effect of (this) repetition in as much as it necessitates the "fading," the obliteration, of the first foundation of the subject, which is why the subject, by status, is always presented as a divided essence";[27] he describes the inverted eight diagram as one that "can be considered the basis of a sort of essential inscription at the origin, in the knot which constitutes the subject";[28] in the context of discourse he says: "In simple terms this only means that in a universe of discourse nothing contains everything, and here you find again the gap that constitutes the subject"[29] and in the context of language he says: "All that is language is lent from this otherness and this is why the subject is always a fading thing that runs under the chain of signifiers."[30] Even as late as 1975 Lacan remained obscure in his consideration of the subject: "How can one sustain a hypothesis such as that of the unconscious, unless one sees that it is the manner in which the subject, if indeed there is such a thing as a subject that is not divided, is impregnated, as it were, by language?"[31] In this lecture the emphasis rests on the link between language and Lacan's understanding of the unconscious, rather than upon the split between the ego and subject. Nevertheless he does not absolutely rule out the concept of "a subject" by way of his divided subject proposition. A divided subject is not synonymous with the idea of two subjects—a divided subject implies one subject who is split rather than two separate subjects.

Because Lacan's postulations are open to varying readings, commentators have come to the position where, either for the sake of clarity or for the sake of attempting to delete logical inconsistencies, they argue the case that in Lacan's theory the individual who speaks to the analyst is best conceptualized in terms of two subjects. E. Bär,[32] for example, divides the subject into subject C (conscious) and subject U (unconscious), claiming that there are degrees in the division of the subject into the two as named. A. Lemaire, too, talks of the subject constituting himself in discourse "by splitting into two parts: subject of the utterance and unconscious subject."[33]

More important, perhaps, is E. Ragland-Sullivan's recent contribution to the field of Lacanian commentaries. In her work *Jacques Lacan and the Philosophy of Psychoanalysis* the author opens chapter 1 entitled "What is I? Lacan's Theory of the Human Subject" with an explanation of the purpose of the chapter as follows: "to establish and explain Lacan's fundamental contention that the human psyche is composed of two different "subjects": an objectlike narcissistic subject of *being* and a *speaking* subject."[34] Throughout this chapter Ragland-Sullivan is at pains not to give the impression of a divided self in everyday terms but stresses that "a symmetrical or binary division cannot be made between the *moi* and the *je* in any case, since both participate in consciousness, in the unconscious, and in an alternating balance of influence."[35]

The *moi* is not susceptible to any one definition, she argues, as she tries to describe and define differences in function and characteristics. The *moi* is not conscious of itself as an object, and yet it occupies a space in consciousness. It is a set of signifying potentials "which never ceases to displace Desire along an endless chain in the incomplete story of identity."[36] The *je* is the "subject of meaning and speech."[37] Her point is that the *moi* and *je* essentially inhabit different realms and are not responsible for the same functions.

In what can be taken as Ragland-Sullivan's attempt to accommodate the problem of the split subject or two subjects, the ego and the subject are primordially linked by "a join both unfathomable and unfixable."[38] The confusing nature of this commentary is, of course, indicative of the difficulty inherent in Lacan's own theory. The very notion of two subjects, joined in some inexplicable or unfathomable way suggests that Lacan's search for a subject leads to the very problem of Freud when in 1919, it will be remembered, he was still bothered by the relationship between the dreamer and his dreams. As noted in chapter 3, Freud concluded that there is "an amalgamation of two separate people who are linked by some important element."[39] The idea of a split subject makes it theoretically necessary to postulate the nature of the link between ego and subject or the conscious subject and the unconscious subject, because we cannot have one without the other. The nature of this link, however, remains an area yet to be adequately theorized.

As I have shown, Lacan's conceptualizations concerning the subject in psychoanalysis change according to the context within which he is working. Overall, however, he does present a case for the notion of a split subject, but he does so more in terms of his idea of the subject as differentiated from the ego than in terms of two subjects as presented by the commentators. With further publication of his Seminar material we will be in a better position to follow his thought regarding the subject in psychoanalysis. Nevertheless it can be said that his stance is not far from that of Freud's account of two separate people who are linked by some important element. Just as Freud never clarified the nature of the link, neither does Lacan. His assertion that the ego is implicated in the structuration of the subject calls for a good deal of explanation. How does this happen? Is the subject also implicated in the structuration of the ego? What is the link between the ego and the symbolic world that is so effectual in the constitution of the subject? The problem of adequately conceptualizing the extremely difficult notion of the subject in psychoanalysis as the speaking being who bears the effect of the Freudian unconscious is perhaps timeless. It is my contention that there is a particularly profitable approach to this problem, one that relies on the introduction of the conceptual tool of structuration. This term is derived in part from the work of Anthony Giddens and is very different from Lacan's use of the term in his Seminars. However, before turning to this idea we need first to focus on the problem of agency in Lacan's work.

The Agency of the Letter in Lacan

Just as Lacan directly addresses the issue of the subject in psychoanalysis so, too, does he directly address the issue of agency within the terms of his own frame of reference. For Lacan, agency pertains to the letter, that is, to the symbolic world or world of signification. This means that for him it is the chain of signifiers endowed with ultimate efficacy that determines the constitution of the subject. Like Freud before him, Lacan separates the concept of subject and the concept of agency. However, whereas Freud failed to clarify his position regarding the status of the subject and imputed agency to the apparatus, Lacan theorizes on the status of the subject but resolutely places the notion of agency within the context of the symbolic world. Lacan makes his point concerning the determination of the subject as follows:

> The concrete, universal discourse, which has been unfolding since the beginning of time. . . . The subject locates himself as such in relation to that, he is inscribed in it, that is how he is already determined, by a determination belonging to a totally different register from that of the determinations of the real, . . . His function, in so far as he continues this discourse, is to rediscover his place in it, not simply as orator, but, here and now, as entirely determined by it.[40]

This central postulate of Lacanian theory—namely, the primacy of the signifier in the constitution of the subject—is presented by Lacan in his quintessential work, the "Seminar on 'The Purloined Letter.' " This piece of work was published in three different forms: as a seminar paper in *Seminar II* in the series edited by Jacques-Alain Miller; as a translation of the original 1956 French essay in *Yale French Studies* 1972–74; and as the opening text in *Écrits,* 1966.[41] This itself is some index of its importance to the theory. In the *Yale French Studies* publication, Lacan's aim in using this classic story is clearly stated as follows:

> . . . to illustrate for you the truth . . . that it is the symbolic order which is constitutive for the subject—by demonstrating in a story the decisive orientation which the subject receives from the itinerary of a signifier.[42]

I want now to recount this story, even though it is possibly well known to those who have had contact with Lacan's work. My need here to retell the story briefly is twofold: first, I want to stress certain aspects of Lacan's reading; and, second, I later want to propose an alternative reading of the story as a means of illustrating a point in my own argument.

The Story

In Edgar Allan Poe's story[43] there are two main scenes. These scenes are introduced by a visit from the prefect of the Parisian police to a certain Dupin, well known to the police for his ability to solve problems. The former tells Dupin of a secret commission that is currently worrying him and describes to him the problem on his hands. The prefect has been commissioned to find a letter that has been stolen from the royal apartment, and his description of how the event took place provides the first scene. The identity of the thief is known, but the whereabouts of the purloined letter remains a mystery. The queen, the prefect explains, had received a letter, and as she perused it was interrupted by the king from whom she wished to keep it concealed. "After a hurried and vain endeavor to thrust it in a drawer, she was forced to place it, open as it was, upon a table."[44] Fortunately for her the king did not notice the letter, which was left with the contents facedown with the address uppermost where it lay. Thereupon another person arrives on the scene, Minister D. As soon as he enters he quickly perceives the situation, he "recognizes the handwriting of the address, observes the confusion of the personage addressed, and fathoms her secret."[45] Before leaving the royal apartment, Minister D takes the queen's letter from the table, leaving another in its place which is of no importance. The queen, who sees the sleight of hand, "dared not call attention to the act, in the presence of the third personage who stood at her elbow."[46] The Prefect of Police explains to Dupin the great efforts that have been made to retrieve the purloined letter, but to no avail. Dupin, being Dupin, later sets out to reclaim the letter without the prefect's knowledge of his action. How he does so provides the second important scene for the story.

Dupin, wearing a pair of green spectacles, visits the minister in the ministerial hotel. He complains of weak eyes as a means of explaining his surveying the apartment with such keenness. On a card rack hanging beneath the mantelpiece he spies a letter, camouflaged by different writing and in a soiled and torn state, which he nonetheless recognizes as being his target. He studies its appearance carefully and, on making his departure leaves a gold snuff box on the table. Dupin returns the next morning having arranged that a pistol shot be fired beneath the windows. As planned, Minister D rushes to the window, unawaredly giving his visitor time to exchange his prepared facsimile for the purloined letter. Dupin regains his snuff box with thanks and leaves.

Lacan's Use of the Story

Lacan uses these two scenes to illustrate the point, among many complex others, that it is the itinerary of the letter that constitutes the position or place of the person. He does this by nominating three places with regard to the letter: (1) the loser, (2) the robber, and (3) the third person, who sees nothing. What is important is how in each scene different persons take those places according to the path of the letter. This can be shown in the following table:

The Loser	The Robber	Third Person
Scene I		
queen	minister	king
Scene II		
minister	Dupin	police (queen)

It is the letter that deals with them; they simply submit to its course and have their acts and destiny determined by it. Lacan asserts: "One can say that, when the characters get hold of this letter, something gets hold of them and carries them along and this something clearly has dominion over their individual idiosyncracies."[47] Perhaps the clearest exposition of his argument is as follows:

> If what Freud discovered and rediscovers with a perpetually increasing sense of shock has a meaning, it is that the displacement of the signifier determines the subjects in their acts, in their destiny, in their refusals, in their blindnesses, in their end and in their fate, their innate gifts and social acquisitions notwithstanding, without regard for character or sex, and that, willingly or not, everything that might be considered the stuff of psychology, kit and caboodle, will follow the path of the signifier.[48]

Such a reading of the Poe story is based on the Lacanian thesis that it is the letter that holds signification for the subject: in other words, that the subject is determined by the signifier. Lacan claims that the letter has

a meaning for the queen and for the minister, that they are directed by
the signification of the letter for them. Because Lacan imputes agency to
the letter, he is able to read the story in the light of the claim that
underpins his psychoanalytic theory. This allows him to bypass what is an
important point in the story—the position of the loser.

The Loser

In Lacan's reading of the story three places are named, one of which is
"the loser." What Lacan bypasses is that in the first scene the loser is a
loser in an *active* sense, whereas in the second scene the loser is so in a
passive sense. When the queen loses the letter to Minister D, she does so
knowingly and actively allows this to take place. However, when the
minister loses the letter to Dupin, he does so totally unawaredly and
therefore passively. To bypass this distinguishing characteristic in the two
scenes seems like a sleight of hand because it allows Lacan to make his
point without a stumble. If one obliterates this difference, then both are
simply determined losers. Yet, it is not the case because another mode of
action is possible for the queen even if she does not choose to carry it out.
There is no choice for Minister D.

I point this out to illustrate what is presumably obvious: that it is
Lacan who gives meaning to this story. The meaning that he provides
supports his argument, which sees the players in the story as being
determined by the agency of the letter. An alternative reading of the Poe
story is possible—one that does not support Lacan's position. I will
return to this point after we have given further consideration to an
impasse to be found in Lacan's theoretical elaborations.

The Agency of the Letter: The Agency of the Subject

If one accepts the Lacanian postulate of the supremacy of the signifier,
then Lacan's subsequent description of the subject in terms of the signifier
is without problem. Subject and agency are acknowledged as being separate terms, and it is the subject who is constituted by the agency of the
letter. In line with this approach are Lacan's descriptions of the subject

such as "the subject is the subject of the signifier—determined by it"[49] or more explicitly:

> The signifier, producing itself in the field of the Other, makes manifest the subject of its signification. But it functions as a signifier only to reduce the subject in question to being no more than a signifier, to petrify the subject in the same movement in which it calls the subject to function, to speak, as subject.[50]

Here the subject is considered by Lacan to be represented by the signifier but to be no more than a signifier. This implies, surely, that there is really no subject, only signification. Yet, surprisingly within the same breath we are told that the subject is called upon to function, to speak. Who is this assumedly active being? Who speaks? Surely the signified subject can only be spoken by the signifier. Lacan does impute agency to the subject because he refers to the subject as the one who speaks as subject. If the subject speaks, then Lacan posits a position that is fundamentally contrary to his deterministic stance. Numerous such contradictions are to be found throughout his teaching where subject and agency are concerned. For example, when discussing the process of analysis, Lacan points out that the subject must enter into a new circle of signifiers. This is tantamount to admitting that the subject is an active agent within the process itself:

> Analysis is made for him to make out, for him to understand in what circle of speech he is caught, and by the same token into what other circle he must enter.[51]

To which subject does Lacan refer here where he speaks of the patient's understanding his/her position in the circuit of signifiers, the conscious subject or the subject of/in the unconscious? In what sense can this subject enter into another circle of signifiers? Is movement a matter of willpower, or is agency imputed to the subject of/in the unconscious? Because the subject is said to understand and what is more has the ability to move from one position to another where the circle of signification is concerned, Lacan imputes this undefined subject with the attribute of agency over the recognized signifying chain. How are we to reconcile theoretically contradictory assumptions concerning the subject in psychoanalysis and the issue of agency? On the one hand, with great definitiveness and authority Lacan imputes agency to the signifier. Yet, on the other hand, he attributes the theoretically necessary concept of agency to the subject in the process of change within the analysis itself.

Even years later, in 1964, when Lacan talks of the effect of interpretation we find the same inherent problem when he says: "What is essential
is that he should see, beyond this signification, to what signifier—to what
irreducible, traumatic, non-meaning—he is, as a subject, subjected."[52] If
the patient sees this, then what is the consequence? Is the conscious
patient the subject or is the subject subject to the unconscious? If the
latter is the case, then how can the unconscious subject be brought to see
to what s/he is subjected and how can the unconscious subject alter his/
her position with regard to the circuit of signifiers? Can the subject
involve him/herself in the reconstitution of desire? What is the nature of
the link between such a recognition as mentioned above and the subject's
existence? Is interpretation simply brilliant technical manipulation of signification, or is the subject involved in any sense actively in the process of
analysis? Lacan takes the position that it is the signifier that determines
the subject, yet when talking of potential for change through the analytic
process itself his foot slips into an alternative position—one that imputes
agency to the subject who can make some alteration to his/her state of
imprisonment in the web of preordained significations.

In *The Four Fundamental Concepts* we find a similar contradiction
where Lacan argues as follows:

> The unconscious is the sum of the effects of speech on a subject, at the level
> at which the subject constitutes himself out of the effects of the signifier.[53]

How can a subject who is determined by the signifier constitute himself?
How can a subject who is structured, who is at the behest of the symbolic
world, who is positioned according to the whim of the signifier also or
simultaneously structure his being? Although Lacan is adamant about and
never rescinds his position regarding the agency of the letter in the
determination of the subject, he can nevertheless write with reference to
the subject: "That is what enables him to *see* in its place and to structure,
as a function of his place and of his world, his being."[54] Lacan is quite
clear in this latter passage that it is the subject who constitutes and
structures his being. Unless one can argue for poor translation, this
proposition is completely and utterly contrary to his position that states
that "the subject is the subject of the signifier—determined by it."[55]

If, as Lacan often writes, the subject is "in fading"[56] because of his/her
subordination to the signifier, it would be theoretically consistent to say
that the subject is spoken by the signifier. Lacan does take this stance, and

it is especially clear where he describes man's relation to the signifier as follows:

> This passion of the signifier now becomes a new dimension of the human condition in that it is not only man who speaks, but that in man and through man *it* speaks *(ça parle)*, that his nature is woven by effects in which is to be found the structure of language, of which he becomes the material, and that therefore there resounds in him, beyond what could be conceived of by a psychology of ideas, the relation of speech.[57]

Consistent with this view is his popularly cited "The signifier . . . represents a subject for another signifier."[58] Here we can see to what extent priority is given to the symbolic world. The subject is referred to only in terms of its relationship to the dominant chain of signifiers, which are themselves invested with agency. The signifiers relate to one another as agents about what might be termed, their object, the subject in psychoanalysis. Lacan distinguishes the signifier from the sign. The latter, he explains, is "something intended for someone."[59] Whereas in the case of a sign, the subject is agent and the sign is an object, in the case of the signifier, the subject is an object and the signifier, the agent.

Lacan can, nevertheless, teach with contrary assumptions. This he does when his stance concerning the subject implies that the subject is an agent, at least where speech is concerned. In the citation to follow it is the subject who speaks, not the signifier. Even if the subject speaks unknowingly, agency rests with the subject and not with the signifier:

> So the Freudian discovery leads us to hear in discourse this speech which reveals itself through, or even in spite of, the subject.
>
> He tells us this speech not only verbally, but through all his other means of expression. Even through his body, the subject emits a speech, which is, as such, speech of truth, a signifying speech which he does not even know he emits. It is because he always says more than he means to, always more than he thinks he says.[60]

Granted the latter quotation is drawn from the 1953–54 Seminar papers whereas the former is culled from the 1958 paper delivered in Munich, but the same inconsistency can be evidenced in Lacan's thinking within the time span of only a matter of weeks. For instance, in March 1955 Lacan can talk in terms of "this speech which is in the subject without being the speech of the subject" and in terms of the usually confusing subject/unconscious problem already mentioned: "there is a beyond to the *ego,* an unconscious, a subject which speaks, unknown to the subject."[61] Here we are told that there is speech that is not speech of the subject, but we do not know how such speech is to be conceptualized, where it is anchored. Then, fourteen days later he opens his Seminar with the question that he has been pursuing: namely, *"What is the subject?"* His answer refers to "the unconscious subject, and by way of that, essentially the subject who speaks." "Now," he continues, "it seems more and more clear to us that this subject who speaks is beyond the *ego.*"[62] Here we find the subject who speaks, not the subject who is spoken, and at this stage he implies that speech is anchored in the subject although this is so unbeknownst to the speaker. My point is that Lacan holds two contradictory assumptions simultaneously: that the subject speaks and that the subject is spoken. The former imputes agency to the subject, the latter imputes agency to the signifier. Much of this problem can be accounted for in terms of the difficulty in understanding what Lacan means by the concept of "subject," but it is further complicated by his ability to impute agency to both signifier and subject at the same time either directly or by implication.

The same logical contradiction concerning the location of agency in the work of Lacan is to be found in the allied problem of the origins of speech. If agency is imputed to the signifier, then it is a theoretical necessity that language preexists man whom it is to structure. If the subject is spoken, then language must necessarily exist, awaiting man's arrival to work its way through him. When pressed about the origin of language in *Seminar II,* Lacan fails to argue a case that is consistent with his stance: "I wasn't trying to tell you that I believed that language was in the beginning—I know nothing of origins."[63] Thus, his stance with regard to the agency of the letter rests on very shaky grounds. Nevertheless Lacan holds that within a "certain perspective" a claim can be made about origins that is in line with the crux of his theory:

> But the question isn't at this point to know whether we should put the word or speech in the beginning. In the perspective we have taken on today and which I just illustrated by Daniel von Chepko's distich, there's a mirage whereby language, namely all your little Os and Is, is there from all eternity, independently of us. You may well ask me—*Where?* I would be really hard pressed finding an answer. But what is certain, as Mannoni [analyst] was

saying earlier on, is that within a certain perspective, we can only see them as being there since the beginning of time.[64]

This "certain perspective" is that which leads to the Poe reading offered by Lacan—one in which Lacan posits that agency pertains to language, not to the individual. Yet Lacan also imputes agency to individuals where the constitution of the symbolic world is concerned: "All human beings share in the universe of symbols. They are included in it and submit to it, much more than they constitute it. They are much more its supports than its agents."[65] Here, although with reticence, Lacan acknowledges the agency of the subject in the constitution of the universe of symbols. Human beings do, indeed, in his own words, constitute the symbolic world even if this is to a lesser degree than they are constituted by it. They are, he admits, agents in its construction.

The "Real Lacan"

Two dimensions of Lacan's tridimensional thinking, referred to in terms of the Symbolic, Imaginary, and Real, have been thrown into relief in the foregoing discussion: namely, the Symbolic and the Imaginary. While in his early years Lacan placed much emphasis on these through his interest in language (Symbolic) and the distinction between the subject and the illusionary ego (Imaginary), he did employ the concept of the Real— though to a lesser extent than in his later formulations. In *Seminar I,* for example, he talks of the Real in terms of its link with the other two dimensions: "The whole problem is that of the juncture of the symbolic and of the imaginary in the constitution of the real."[66] This juncture he represents topographically with the three-faceted Borromean knot. The significance of this tridimensional thinking to his theory construction is clear in his comment: "It is within the dimension of being that the tripartition of the symbolic, the imaginary and the real is to be found, those elementary categories without which we would be incapable of distinguishing anything within our experience."[67] In the fifties Lacan was concerned with the question of being and its place within psychoanalytic theory, but in his later years he repudiated this path. Although we will return to this concept ourselves in the chapter to follow, what is important here is not so much his attention to being but his tridimensional psychoanalytic framework. In other words, from his early to his later years of theory construction, Lacan proposed a tridimensional mode of thought. For him, psychoanalytic thinking necessarily entails the use of these interdependent concepts.

One of the most lucid commentators on Lacan's thought is the philosopher Slavoj Žižek. In his work *The Sublime Object of Ideology* (1989)[68] he points out that in the 1950s Lacan referred to the Real in terms of the brute, presymbolic reality, whereas in the 1970s the use of the concept approaches more and more what in the 1950s Lacan called the Imaginary. In a sense, we could say that Lacan's use of the concept of the Real became more and more abstract. Although the Real refers to that dimension where nothing is lacking (lack is introduced by symbolization), as well as to the gap, the hole around which the symbolic order is structured, it is also said not to exist. Rather, Žižek explains, the Real has a series of properties and exercises a certain structural causality. Thus, it is said that although it does not exist, it is nevertheless able to produce a series of effects in the symbolic reality of the subject. It is not my intention here to discuss Lacan's use of the Real in any detail. It is important, however, to acknowledge that in his later years his theory construction was tackled with an accent on the idea of the Real rather than with an accent on the Symbolic as seen in our discussion of his earlier work.

This change in emphasis brought with it an alteration in Lacan's approach to the subject. Whereas in his initial postulations the subject is conceptualized as an empty place in which his or her whole content is procured by others, by the symbolic network of intersubjective relations, in his last works there is a possibility for "the subject to obtain some contents." Žižek explains this as follows:

> But Lacan's basic thesis, at least in his last works, is that there is a possibility for the subject to obtain some contents, some kind of positive consistency, also outside the big Other, the alienating symbolic network. This other possibility is that offered by fantasy: equating the subject to an object of fantasy.[69]

If the subject is an object of fantasy, how are we to understand at a theoretical level the notion of the one who constructs the fantasy? From first to last, Lacan seems reticent to broach this issue. His theory requires an active subject, but his definitions of the subject are constantly those that refer to an emptiness or an object. His subject is always one that is ultimately devoid of agency.

A change in his conceptualization of the subject is evident where he uses the paradigm of a question and answer. Lacan, with his emphasis on the notion of the Real, defines the subject as "an answer of the Real."[70] An answer to what, we might query? To the question asked by the Symbolic, Lacan teaches. We can immediately see that the subject is subject to the dimensions of his theoretical framework, to the Real and the Symbolic. The subject is not actively engaged but is a passive recipient to and a product of a life-endowed conceptual framework. Lacan's argument is that the subject is to be conceptualized as an answer, the subject is not a question, the subject does not ask a question—the subject is an answer of the Real. Nevertheless, and this is a crucial point for our argument, at this time, just as in his earlier work, it is the Symbolic that is imputed with agency. Lacan holds that the subject is an answer of the Real to the question asked by the Other, that is the symbolic order. Thus, irrespective of new or different emphases, Lacan never moves from his original position where he argues that the subject is subject to the signifier.

In this later formulation of Lacan, the subject neither asks nor answers the question—it is the symbolic order that asks the question, and it is from the Real that the answer comes forth. In the light of such a theoretical formulation we could say that the Symbolic and Real are anthropomorphized (as was the psychic apparatus in Freud), while the subject is a vehicle for their intercourse. The point is, in any case, that the subject in the later work of Lacan is constituted via the Other. Agency is located in the Other, and it is separate from the concept of the subject in psychoanalysis.

This question-answer paradigm is extended in Lacan's theory construction to include the key concept, *object a*. Again, there is no need for us to concern ourselves with this formulation other than in passing. Lacan postulates that *object a* is the true object of the question. This concept, one that is fundamental to his theory of the desiring subject, he now defines in terms of the Real. It is, among other things, the point of the Real "in the heart of the subject which cannot be symbolized."[71] It is that which is produced as a residue, a remnant, a leftover of every signifying operation. Yet, even with the introduction of the concept *object a* within the question-answer paradigm, Lacan's teaching is essentially unchanged. He postulates that agency resides elsewhere other than in the subject.

From whatever aspect of his tridimensional framework he speaks, Lacan holds that from a theoretical perspective, the subject is subject to the symbolic. The subject is conceptualized as a passive recipient and product of a surrounding and dominant trimodal structure.

However, it is also the case that when Lacan is especially interested in the Real, he nevertheless does employ the idea of an active agent. Žižek explains that, for Lacan, the subject is "an active agent, the bearer of some signification who is trying to express himself in language."[72] Yet, as always, this aspect of agency, here denoted by self-expression, is overridden by the agency imputed to the symbolic. Lacan's starting point throughout his entire *oeuvre* is that the symbolic representation always distorts the subject—it is always a displacement, a failure. The subject, Lacan teaches, cannot find a signifier that is his or her own. Žižek relates:

> The subject of the signifier is precisely this lack, this impossibility of finding a signifier which would be "its own": the failure of its *representation is its positive condition*. The subject tries to articulate itself in a signifying representation; the representation fails; instead of a richness we have a lack, and this void opened by the failure *is* the subject of the signifier.[73]

Here we seem to be closer to the clinical situation—one where the subject speaks to the analyst—because this conceptualization is derived from the perspective of the Symbolic rather than from the Real. Although the latter has clinical implications, the subject as subject of the signifier is certainly the subject who tries to articulate him or herself in a signifying representation. Yet, there are still the same unresolved issues regarding subject and agency.

When Lacan imputes some degree of agency to the subject—an attempt to express him/herself through speech—how are we to understand this subject? Is this a conscious intention, one that requires the effort of a conscious subject? Or, is this the action of the subject of the unconscious? Presumably so, because that is the subject as defined in Lacanian psychoanalysis. Yet, who is the subject that tries to express him/herself quite purposefully? In other words, how are we to conceptualize the subject of what Lacan refers to as empty speech? Is there an agent of such speech? What is the relationship between this subject, if there is one, and the subject who endeavors to express him/herself but must of necessity fail. The 'I' of conscious discourse might be said to be but indicative of the subject who speaks, that is, designates the subject without being able to signify it, but who is the agent of that intended 'I'? Who accepts or rejects what is revealed from the discourse of the unconscious in the analytic situation? Indeed, who acknowledges the truth of the unconscious? Who is it that can say, "Yes, that is true of me but I had no idea of it at all"? In his early years and in his later work Lacan constantly bypasses these crucial clinical issues.

Conclusion

We have seen that in Lacan's theoretical work the concept of agency and the concept of the subject have been separated. For Lacan, agency is imputed to the signifier and it is the signifier that determines the subject. This is so throughout his entire teaching irrespective of whether his psychoanalytic thought is based upon one or other of his tridimensions, the Symbolic, Imaginary, and Real. Nevertheless, although this conceptualization of agency is a tenet within his teaching, we have found a number of instances where Lacan's propositions rest on a contrary assumption—namely, that agency is located in the subject. Elsewhere we have found that owing to his emphasis on the subject of the unconscious, Lacan has been able to bypass other issues of subject and agency. How, for example, might we conceptualize the subject of consciousness—that is, the agent of intended speech. How and in what way is this agent distinct from the illusionary ego?

This means that although Lacan addresses the problem found in the work of Freud, Hartmann, and Klein—namely, that they did not clarify the nature of their theoretical assumptions concerning the agency of the subject in the clinical context—we are still left with a number of crucial unresolved issues. Because our focus is on the subject who speaks to the analyst, our reading of Lacan leaves us with many questions but perhaps with one that is most pressing. This question is central to any psychoanalytic theory that deals with what Freud has referred to as "the magical power of words."[74] It is the Humpty-Dumpty question: the question posed by Humpty Dumpty when he and Alice discuss this very issue of subject, agency, and speech:

> "When *I* use a word," Humpty Dumpty said in rather an scornful tone, "it means just what I choose it to mean—neither more nor less."

"The question is," said Alice, "whether you *can* make words mean different things."

"The question is," said Humpty Dumpty, "which is to be master—that's all."[75]

In theory, Lacan answers definitively that the signifier is master and the subject is slave. In practice, however; his feet are in two places at once. We might ask, then, what are the implications of the alternative stance, one that posits the idea that the subject is master of language rather than its slave? Again, we might ask: Is the answer to Humpty Dumpty's question necessarily one or the other of these stances? Could it be that Humpty Dumpty and ourselves ask the wrong question? To answer the first of these questions (I will focus on the second in the next chapter), I would like to return to the Poe story and suggest a possible alternative reading of the material. In this reading the human being is the master, for it is based on the claim that it is not the signifier that gives meaning to the subject but rather that it is the subject who gives meaning to the signifier.

An Alternative Reading of the Poe Story

In the first scene, you will remember, the queen is flustered with regard to a letter in her possession. She has been unable to conceal this letter, which lies upon a table within the range of the view of the king and Minister D. Given the alternative claim, that the human being is master of language, the queen could be said to give signification to this letter by virtue of the meaning that she constructs concerning its presence in her life. Without the activity of her being flustered, which is a direct consequence of the meaning that she constructs, the letter would probably have been given little significance by the minister and so never *have been set in play by him*. The letter does not have a life of its own but is given life through the meaning imputed to it by the players. From the minister's point of view the queen's behavior gives him reason to suppose that the letter is of importance, and so it is given meaning by him—he constructs a story about the letter to provide a motive for the queen's panic and being flustered. Because of the meaning that he attributes to the letter, he sets about stealing it—and so the circuit is put into action. There would

be no circuit if the players were not actively involved both in the construction of signification and in the activity that is in line with the varying
meanings attributed to people and events. The letter does not fly through
the air—it is carried by those who give it a meaning, one that necessitates
some form of consequent action. The reader of the story does not know
the contents of the letter, but for each character its significance changes
according to the meaning given it by the particular person involved in the
play.

In the second scene, Dupin spies the letter in Minister D's apartment.
Dupin thinks that the letter provides the means of consolidating his
reputation for solving problems; he steals it by means of returning a
second time with a facsimile and makes the necessary exchange. The
meaning of the letter in this scene changes according to whom one
perceives as being the actor involved. Dupin constructs a meaning in line
with his need to maintain a reputation; Minister D constructs a meaning
in line with his motivations.

Clearly this reading of the Poe story does not rely on the Lacanian
thesis that man is submitted to the agency of the letter. It assumes that
the letter is submitted to the agency of the human being, the subject. The
real point here is that the same material can be read with different
assumptions underpinning the reading. It is not a question of which is
right and which is wrong but much more a case of which reading is the
more productive at the level of theory construction. I have argued that
Lacan's assumption concerning the signifier as agent brings him to a
theoretical impasse. The alternative reading, however, does little more
than bring us full circle to the problem that faced Freud in the case of the
hystérique d'occasion. If agency is imputed to the subject, then why is it that
this woman could not feed her baby as she so much wanted to do? To
impute agency to the subject is to deny the very essence of the Freudian
discovery—namely, the existence of the unconscious.

This leaves us with the further question: Is the answer to Humpty
Dumpty's question necessarily one or the other? That is, is there need to
conceptualize the subject as either master or slave where language is
concerned? In the chapter to follow I will put forward a case that over-
rides the problem of the attribution of agency to the subject, to the
psychic apparatus, or to language. What I propose is that a completely
different type of claim be made where the concept of subject and language
is concerned, one that necessitates turning to the field of social theory to

gain from the work of Anthony Giddens. Here I do not ask, like Hartmann, what we can offer the field of sociology, but rather what Giddens' social theory can offer to the problem that I have identified as being at the center of psychoanalytic theory construction—namely, the separation of the concepts of subject and agency.

A PROPOSED SOLUTION

8

A Conceptual Tool of Structuration

The Problem

This book argues that underlying Freud's theory of the psychic apparatus is an implicit division between the concept of agency and the concept of the subject. As a consequence of this division, we have seen that although both Hartmann and Klein adopt the Freudian topography—and make structural changes to it—each makes radically different assumptions as to how the subject in psychoanalysis is to be conceptualized. In the case of Lacan's theory, the notion of the subject and the notion of agency are likewise dealt with as separate concepts. In the last chapter we explored the way in which this separation of concepts leads to inconsistency in Lacan's theoretical formulations.

Irrespective of these inconsistencies and irrespective of the problems for theory construction that ensue from his idea of the split subject, Lacan has redirected the Freudian discovery toward the link between the subject in psychoanalysis and language. This is of major importance because the focus of his work rests upon the idea of the subject—that is, the subject who speaks to the analyst. No other psychoanalytic theoretician has given such weight to the domain of language and the constitution of the subject. With regard to the importance of speech in clinical practice, for example, Lacan explains:

> . . . for some years all my effort has been required in a struggle to bring to the attention of these practitioners the true value of this instrument, *speech* —to give it back its dignity, so that it does not always represent for them

151

those words, devalued in advance, that focus them to fix their gaze elsewhere, in order to find their guarantor.[1]

It is this emphasis on the subject, understood in terms of the being who
speaks, that I hold to be of prime importance within the framework of
the theory and practice of psychoanalysis. Psychoanalysis works with
words, words spoken by a subject who asks that the analyst listen to him
or her within confines of the analytic session. How, then, can the notion
of subject and of agency best be handled at a theoretical level where an
emphasis on language is maintained? Given that a separation between the
concepts of subject and agency has been shown to produce problems for
psychoanalytic theory, what is needed is a conceptual tool that will handle
those difficulties that have been discussed in the foregoing chapters. Put
succinctly, what is needed is a conceptual tool that

1. avoids a division between the concepts of subject and agency;
2. allows us to retain the emphasis on speech which is held to be
   central to the concept of the subject in psychoanalysis;
3. overcomes the impasse that is a result of the attribution of agency
   to either the subject or to language.

One possible avenue for us to take at this point is to turn to the work
of Anthony Giddens, a world-renowned scholar and theoretician in the
field of the social sciences. Although Giddens's work does not bear at all
directly on the problem posed in terms of subject and agency, his theory
of structuration can be adapted to provide the means of finding a solution
to the issue that I claim besets psychoanalytic theory construction. In the
first section of this chapter I will introduce Giddens's theory within the
context to which it belongs—namely, social theory—then suggest the
way in which the conceptual tool of structuration might be profitably
applied to the notions of subject and language within the domain of
psychoanalysis. It is via this route that we will find that Humpty Dumpty's question becomes irrelevant. "Which is to be master"—subject or
language? My response to Humpty is to say that he asks the wrong
question, for, given the use of the concept of structuration as I propose it
in this chapter, there is no question of power, control, or agency. Subject
and language are, rather, proposed as interdependent concepts within the
framework of a dual structure. As a means of clarifying the potential of
the concept of structuration I will apply the proposed tool to a current
problem in psychoanalytic theory: the problem of the relationship be-

tween subject, language, and sexual difference. At this point it is my intention to do no more than introduce the new concept and to provide an instance of the way in which it can be employed. The prime importance of the term *structuration* in the present context is that it copes with those issues that have been delineated as difficulties for psychoanalytic theory construction. Last, both subject and psychic apparatus will be discussed in the light of the proposal made.

Giddens's Theory of Structuration

Anthony Giddens is a Fellow of King's College and Professor of Sociology at the University of Cambridge, England. He is the author[2] of numerous books on social theory including *Capitalism and Modern Social Theory, The Class Structure of the Advanced Societies, New Rules of Sociological Method,* and *Social Theory and Modern Sociology.* In *Central Problems in Social Theory: Action, Structure and Contradiction in Social Analysis,* Giddens proposes what he terms a theory of structuration by means of which he handles the problem of structure and agent in an innovative yet logically consistent and coherent way.

Although Giddens does use the term *theory* in reference to the concept of structuration, I think the term is more appropriately referred to as a conceptual tool that he employs in his social theory. Giddens never expounds his theory of structuration but comprehensively defines the term in one paragraph as follows:

> The concept of structuration involves that of the *duality of structure, which relates to the fundamentally recursive character of social life, and expresses the mutual dependence of structure and agency.* By the duality of structure I mean that the structural properties of social systems are both the medium and the outcome of the practices that constitute those systems. The theory of structuration, thus formulated, rejects any differentiation of synchrony and diachrony or statics and dynamics. The identification of structure with constraint is also rejected: structure is both enabling and constraining, and it is one of the specific tasks of social theory to study the conditions in the organization of social systems that govern the interconnections between the two. According to this conception, the same structural characteristics participate in the subject (the actor) as in the object (society). Structure forms 'personality' and 'society' simultaneously—but in neither case exhaustively: because of the significance of unintended consequences of action, and

because of unacknowledged conditions of action. Ernst Bloch says, *Homo semper tiro:* man is always a beginner. We may agree, in the sense that every process of action is a production of something new, a fresh act; but at the same time all action exists in continuity with the past, which supplies the means of its initiation. *Structure thus is not to be conceptualised as a barrier to action, but as essentially involved in its production:* even in the most radical processes of social change which, like any others, occur in time. The most disruptive modes of social change, like the most rigidly stable forms, involve structuration.[3]

The importance of this term within his theory is best understood by seeing it at work at the level of his macrotheory. His focus of interest is the subject and society and the nature of the relationship between the two. The issue that concerns him relates to Humpty Dumpty's question as to which is master. For Giddens, however, the question does not concern subject and language as it does for Humpty Dumpty and for us; instead, it concerns subject and society. Is the subject master of society or is society master of the subject? In other words, where is the concept of agency best located? Giddens's answer is that agency is to be found in neither the subject nor in society. His innovation is to theorize in such a way that he avoids the problem of agency altogether. Thus, he shows us that the question need not even be asked. Giddens dismantles the division between the concepts of subject and society and in the process makes the concept of agency superfluous. This he does by his use of the concepts of subject and society as *interdependent* rather than as separate notions.

We need to be careful here not to think in terms of interaction. Interaction refers to the inter-action of two separate variables. The variables involved in this process are not dependent on each other for their own existence—they can stand alone, and each could be involved with some other variable altogether. *Interactive variables* come together to *produce a particular process* that is dependent on them for its existence. Interdependent variables, however, require each other for their very being; neither can stand alone. It is the *process of interdependency* itself that is *productive of both variables,* and without this process neither variable can be said to exist. Giddens proposes the idea of a subject-society duality; thus neither subject nor society is to be understood as a separate concept. Each is said to rely on the other for its being and only comes into existence via the interdependent process at work.

This means that in the terms of his work both society and the subject are each considered medium and outcome of that which constitutes the social world. Because society and subject are essentially interdependent aspects of the social system itself, neither can be said to be the agent where the other is concerned. Both are involved in what Giddens refers to as a process of structuration—a process that relies on the dynamic of recursivity. It is the introduction of this term that makes the concept of agency irrelevant to his postulation. In Giddens's theory the two components that are held to be in an interdependent recursive relation with each other are the subject, usually taken to be the agent in social theory, and society, usually understood in terms of object. The idea of recursivity means that the designations of subject and society are no longer to be understood as subject and object but as mutually dependent variables involved in a process of interdependent recursivity. It is by virtue of the recursive nature of the process that neither subject nor society can be considered to be the "agent." The subject works through society, and society works through the subject by means of the recursive process at play—a process that involves both and is productive of both. By employing the concept of recursivity, Giddens is able to collapse the usually assumed separation of subject and society and at the same time avoid the use of the notion of agency with its "either-or" implications as far as subject and society are concerned. Both subject and society are equally implicated in an ongoing process that takes each to be simultaneously medium and outcome of a *duality of structure*.

However, in Giddens's consideration although the separation between the concepts has been lost, a new element is to be recognized and acknowledged. This element concerns the idea of a dual structure. Because society and subject are mutually dependent, they share in the same structuration process and therefore the same structural characteristics. What this means is that the structural properties that pertain to the subject also pertain to society.

Margaret Archer[4] has rightly criticized Giddens's work on the basis of his conflating the two components in structuration—in his case, subject and society. She has suggested using the strategy of analytical dualism in order to isolate the relative influence of either in any given moment of the structuration process. What is important for us in her view, and what we will follow, is her proposal that each component is to be understood to have its own logical properties while nonetheless being conceptualized within a duality. Thus she is critical of Giddens's idea that the same structural properties pertain to both subject and society.

Structuration in Psychoanalytic Theory

If we apply the concept of structuration to the problem at hand, we are provided with the leverage necessary to work at a theoretical level with both subject and language where neither is to be considered agent or object, master or slave. Just as Giddens is able to bypass the conceptual separation between subject and society by proposing a duality of structure, so, too, are we now able to eradicate the conceptual separation between subject and agency. We can do this by introducing the idea of a duality of structure to psychoanalytic theory not as in Giddens's work between subject and society, but between subject and language. Now, rather than talk in terms of subject and language as separate concepts, we can conceptualize subject and language in terms of a dual structure. This means that we now consider the terms *subject* and *language* as components within the process of structuration—a process that involves the key notion of recursivity. Thus, subject and language are both medium and outcome of a dual structure. Both components are recognized as different and can be investigated separately for heuristic purposes alone, but each is held to be essential to the other *within the process of structuration*. Just as the subject as medium produces the outcome where language is concerned, so too is language the medium and produces the outcome where the constitution of the subject is concerned. Whereas Lacan considers the latter aspect of the proposed duality with disregard for the former, it is my argument that both must be taken into account simultaneously. This can only be done where the duality is taken as a fundamental notion. The concept of agency is automatically superfluous to this new conceptualization because subject and language are understood by their very nature to be involved in a process of recursivity. Neither language nor subject is understood to be master, thus neither is imputed with agency. By eradicating the idea of agency altogether through the introduction of the idea of recursivity, we have a conceptualization at hand that overcomes the problems that have emerged in our investigation. What we now have is the idea of the subject and language being both medium and outcome of each other simultaneously, where subject and language are understood within the context of a dual structure, each expressing, through the process of recursivity, their mutual dependence. Thus, by means of the introduction of the concept of structuration into psychoanalytic theory

(1) the division between the concepts of subject and agency is overcome; (2) the emphasis on language is ensured; and (3) neither subject nor language is imputed with agency.

As a means of presenting this new idea, I want at this point to illustrate the way in which the concept of structuration can be seen to be useful when applied to a current problem in psychoanalytic theory. I will do this by way of presenting a critique of a recent work by a notable Lacanian, Stuart Schneiderman. My primary aim here is to present the concept of structuration at *work,* and in so doing I will endeavor to make this as-yet-unknown notion as accessible as I can to the reader. It is not so much that I wish to criticize Schneiderman's contribution but rather that I want to use the issue he raises and the assertions he makes as a vehicle to expound upon my own proposal.

An Application of the Concept of Structuration to a Current Problem in Psychoanalytic Theory

Stuart Schneiderman is a Lacanian analyst and author of several books[5] and numerous articles within the Lacanian tradition. In his recent work *An Angel Passes: How the Sexes Became Undivided,*[6] he addresses a central issue for psychoanalysis: namely, the relationship between the world of words and sexual difference. Following Lacan, Schneiderman imputes agency to the world of words and does so in what might be referred to as a somewhat blatant manner:

> Our position is that the interaction of the elements of the sentence or sentences, defines and determines the interaction of those who deploy them. Sentences, in other words, do not always do what you think they are doing; they do not always ply themselves to your will. Words are not a possession of humans; they have better things to do than to bow down in obedience to any human subject.[7]

The route that Schneiderman takes to present his case, although interesting and intellectually engaging, leads him to provide an account of the difference between the Christian tradition and psychoanalysis rather than to present an adequate account of his intended project. This Schneiderman designates as being concerned with angels. He proposes that angels who are "invisible spirits who fly through the air bearing messages have a very close resemblance to spoken words."[8] Thus, he claims that by hypostatizing spoken words as invisible flying messengers, "we are thereby permitted to visualize the operation of language."[9] The advantage of employing the celestial beings is, in his words, that it would "provide an account of how the world of words, taken to be abstract, is mapped onto the world of humans—how in other words, the structure of language intersects with and determines the structure of human relations."[10] Perhaps argument by analogy is dangerous at any time. In this case it seems somewhat to limit Schneiderman in that although he provides an interesting account of selected aspects of the Christian tradition, in particular the Catholic Church, it is only in his last two chapters that he seriously addresses the issue of sexual difference and proposes a linguistic theoretical approach to the problem posed. I will move to these last chapters now, leaving aside those that preceed them, as only the former are of immediate concern to my stated aim.

In line with his stance that it is language that determines the subject, Schneiderman works on the assumption that it is language or the world of words, that structures sexual difference. His task is to provide a theoretical rationale as to how this takes place. Again, Schneiderman calls on Lacan to give direction to his thought: "Lacan has stated that the signifier enters the world through sex."[11] Schneiderman proceeds to draw from this the implication that

> the question of how language comes to function in the world, how it hooks into the world, to use the phrase of Hilary Putnam, is addressed through an appreciation of the sexual division of the human race. Language hooks into its speakers in dividing them.[12]

In the chapters entitled "Manliness" and "Femininity" he sets about to theorize on how this might be so.

First, he holds that "masculinity is the drama of proper naming"[13] and that, by being named, a man is marked in the sense of being tied to his name inextricably. Of course this leads to a problem where women are concerned especially in light of their change of name at marriage or keeping their maiden name after marriage. Schneiderman attempts to resolve this problem by making a number of suggestions inclusive of the idea that a woman's name does not mark her definitively, "but in a transitory way."[14] Because of Schneiderman's emphasis on the determining power of language, he defines masculinity in linguistic rather than biological terms. Fatherhood, for example, is defined in terms of the act of naming. When describing the psychoanalytic theory of castration, he explains the concept in terms of a symbolic punishment inflicted on a boy as the price of his incestuous desire for his mother: "The consequence is that his contribution to the production of a child is not comprised of sexual material; *he becomes a father by the act of naming his child, of marking him symbolically.*"[15] With regard to the masculine prerogative of naming, the assumption of the independent and determining potency of the world of words plays out in Schneiderman's argument that "the body is the site in which language hooks onto the world through the function of the proper name. The interwining *[sic]* of language and a human being produces a mark on the body, and this mark shows that the human is subjected to the proper name."[16] How this hooking onto or intertwining takes place is never attended to at a theoretical level; yet this postulated process is pivotal to the linguistic approach that Schneiderman advocates with regard to the division of the sexes.

In addition to naming, Schneiderman introduces the idea of the relationship between masculinity and performance: "Being a man involves knowing what has to be done and then doing it."[17] Again, one wonders why this does not pertain to the acts of a woman. Where Schneiderman heads with this assertion is toward the proposition that masculine is related to mover, feminine to being moved. This is in line with his linguistically based assertion that "in a sense there is a sexual division between the performance and the audience of the Homeric epic; the former is masculine and the latter feminine."[18] Toward the end of this chapter Schneiderman finally states his hypothesis, one on which much of the content of his preceeding chapters is based:

> My hypothesis is that a linguistic structure hooks into the human body through the division of the sexes. The reason for this choice is that the division of the sexes provides a visual representation of an interaction that is otherwise invisible. It also tells us that whatever goes on between the subject and predicate in a sentence, or between a speaker and listener when those roles are differentiated, is of the order of the erotic. The point at which the link is made is the male sexual organ.[19]

The chapter on femininity sets out to argue that "femininity is gained only through a woman's interaction with the opposite in a relation of contiguity excluding substitution and similarity."[20] Schneiderman's attempt to define femininity is lost in his presentation, but he does posit some very interesting and thought-provoking ideas. In the last two chapters he claims that a boy becomes a man through an action in which he is marked, whereas "a girl becomes a woman by being moved,"[21] that is, by assuming the structure of the marital exchange which is fundamental to the operative framework. Here Schneiderman follows the Lacanian tenet that the sexual relation is not symmetrical or equal. Furthermore, "Desire comes from without, not within. And masculinity has everything to do with this desire."[22] Thus Schneiderman can posit that "the lack manifested in desire maps onto the female body. The desire 'enmattered' here corresponds to something movable whose mover is outside of it."[23] To bring this into the linguistic framework that he is pursuing, Schneiderman contends that desire can be said to "represent a predicate or a series of predicates in search of a signifier . . ."[24] The signifier that imparts movement is the phallus.

In a nutshell, the basis of Schneiderman's argument is that the division of the sexes is a visual representation of the workings of dialogue. If subject and predicate and speaker and listener are said to be representative of the masculine and feminine positions, then some rationale is needed as to why this is held to be so. Schneiderman notes that there is no distinction between men and women where the faculty of speech is concerned nor is there anatomical distinction of organs of speech and hearing that would lead to this division. He proposes—but points to the weakness of the argument—that a link can be made on the basis of something akin to a resemblance between the emitting or extruding and the function of the male sexual organ, alongside the resemblance between the receptivity of the ears and the receptivity of the female genitals. His own reasoning in support of this mapping is as follows:

> Assume that what goes on in the speech act, in the commerce between speaker and listener, is not very easy to grasp because it works at a level that is fundamentally invisible. Something may be happening in speech, but you do not see how the words do whatever they do. Imagine that in order to get a handle on the workings of dialogue it is necessary to find a visual representation of it. If the two positions—speaker and listener—are divided, then the requirement is to find a visible principle of division that applies, either to the world or to those who use language. If the latter choice is the only one that hooks language into those who use it, it seems that the anatomical difference of the sexes becomes enlisted to provide a visible support for the invisible process. As far as dividing the world is

concerned, the Greeks used *herms* for this purpose. In both cases the key to the mapping is the phallus.[25]

Schneiderman rests his reasoning on the Lacanian thesis that it is the signifier that determines the subject. Yet given that he endeavors to provide a visible representation of an invisible phenomenon, an alternative argument can be proposed to deal with exactly the same material. We are no doubt rightly reminded here of the alternative reading of the Poe story proposed earlier. Schneiderman suggests that in order to get a handle on the workings of dialogue, it is necessary to find a visual representation of it. Based on the alternative thesis that man expresses himself through language, one could suggest that the division of the sexes is represented in the world of language by the distinctions between subject and predicate and between speaker and listener found in the workings of dialogue. From this perspective what is visible corresponds to the invisible structure of dialogue, but here it is the human being that takes the position of agent and language—the position of outcome. Schneiderman lays himself open to this possible criticism of his theory because his reasoning is based on an underlying correspondence theory. This means that according to his reasoning, there is an assumed one-to-one correspondence between two sets of elements—in this case, between the workings of dialogue and sexual difference. There are two interrelated problems with his argument. First, because one element in one set is said to correspond to an element in a second set, the problem with this proposition concerns the issue of agency. In which set (or sets) is agency to be located? Second, although it might be theoretically profitable to point to an observable correspondence between elements and then theorize on the processes that produce the proposed correspondence, Schneiderman poses the correspondence itself using visible and invisible elements but says nothing about the nature of the processes that link the two sets. These problems require elaboration.

Schneiderman's Correspondence Theory

Schneiderman's claim is that the principles dividing speaker and listener and subject and predicate seem to require some way to hook into the human body and some way of being mapped onto a fundamentally visible division of the human species. It would appear that the invisible world of these structures is mapped isomorphically onto a difference between human beings that is visible on the level of genital anatomy.[26]

What is never really clear is whether Schneiderman refers to sex or to gender; but it does seem that it is the anatomical distinction of sexual difference, rather than gender difference, that is his main interest where the subject/language correspondence is the focus of his theoretical thought. The notion of an isomorphic mapping proposed by Schneiderman implies a likeness in form (see the Concise Oxford Dictionary definition *isos:* equal; morphous, having the property of crystallizing in same or closely related geometric forms) and that it is this likeness that is mapped from one onto the other. What this means is difficult to understand where form is concerned given the anatomy of the human being and the structure of dialogue. Apart from this loose use of the word *isomorphic,* what is really at issue is a problem connected with the designation of agent and outcome where correspondence theory is concerned. It is one thing to observe a one-to-one correspondence between two sets of elements, but it is an entirely different argument to propose that one element in one set has some type of causal relationship with an element in another. Given his argument "that the invisible world of these structures (language) is mapped isomorphically onto a difference between human beings that is visible on the level of genital anatomy,"[27] Schneiderman's correspondence theory suggests either that language shapes man's anatomy, which is more than dubious because it implies a causal relationship where language is imputed with agency, or that there are differences found in the structures of dialogue and differences in the anatomy of human beings and that there is an invisible link between the two.

In the latter case, all that can be said is that Schneiderman posits an example of a one-to-one correspondence between two elements in one domain and two elements in another domain with nothing more than the notion of correspondence itself to provide the assumed association. We are left to ponder the usefulness of this type of statement. If there is no more than correspondence postulated, where can that take us from a theoretical point of view? One could just as easily argue that the difference between the hand and the foot provides a visible support for the invisible processes that take place when language is in use. This argument rests on an assumed correspondence, this time between the anatomical distinction between hand and foot and subject and predicate or speaker and listener. It has as much logical validity as that employed by Schneiderman. All we can say is that the link is invisible but claim that it exists. Because Schneiderman talks in terms of an isomorphic mapping but fails to explain precisely what he means by this term, we can do little else than suppose he argues his case from a Lacanian stance. If words have "something like a mind of their own"[28] and the structure of language maps onto the difference between the sexes, we could suppose some type of efficacy on the part of language where the link between dialogue and sexual difference is concerned; yet this idea is completely sidestepped in his presentation. Schneiderman does not specifically mention a causal argument. Rather he claims that the invisible requires a visible representation but fails to provide a convincing rationale as to why these two particular sets are linked and as to how this is so.

Interestingly, he never makes clear the meaning of his statement that the key to the mapping is the phallus. Nor does he elaborate on how the phallus is involved; his attention rests with the notion of structured isomorphic mapping. Yet if the phallus is understood to be the major signifier, then the idea of the phallus giving meaning to anatomical difference would seem to provide a plausible route for theory construction. I will return to this point later.

The assumed conceptual division between the world of words and the subject does trouble Schneiderman irrespective of his espoused Lacanian position. A lengthy paragraph within his Introduction raises the issue, and he acknowledges that confusion abounds. If messenger (subject) and message (language) are separate, what is the nature of the relationship between them? How are language and the subject linked? Because of his Lacanian emphasis on the determining power of the symbolic world, Schneiderman is left to deal with the effect of maintaining a conceptual separation between the subject and language. His way of overcoming this problem is to speculate on the idea of an axis that links speaker and the world of words:

> While we may abstract the world of words and study it in itself, the angels are not just words; they are speakers or users of language. They are not just messages, but they are also messengers. Before concluding that there is something wrong and confused about this, we will say that the world of words, the world of the sentences, cannot be comprised by discussing what

goes on among the words, that it is impossible to make sense of the structure of language without finding a place among the words for the speaker of that language. There may be, . . . , an axis of combination and an axis of selection in the construction of a sentence. But do these two axes hold together without a third axis, moving in a different direction, *an axis that links speaker and language?*[29]

Here Schneiderman rightly raises the issue of how the subject is implicated in his thesis. No doubt we must ask how there can be a world of words without taking into account, *at the same time,* the speaker of these words. At the outset of his book Schneiderman puts forward the idea of an axis that links speaker and language, but all he does within his thesis is to use the phrase "hooks into" or "hooks onto" without providing us with any form of elaboration as to its meaning. To state that language "hooks into" man does not provide an explanation of the phrase let alone give us any understanding of how the process occurs.

We see, then, that there are two main problems to be dealt with in Schneiderman's linguistic approach to the division of the sexes: (1) the inherent logical difficulties in the use of a correspondence theory and (2) the inadequacy of his explanation as to the relationship between the human being and language. Both problems are directly related to the very issue that we have been dealing with in regard to the conceptual separation between subject and language in psychoanalytic theory. In the former instance we are faced with the problem of where the notion of agency is best imputed and in the latter with the problem of how we conceptualize the relationship between subject and language. Schneiderman's attempt to theorize on the crucial area of sexual difference within the psychoanalytic domain, although of the utmost importance in itself, is beset by what I have shown to be a core problem in theory construction for those who work within the Freudian tradition.

If, however, we bring the newly proposed concept of structuration to bear upon this issue, we have the means of addressing it from a very different vantage point. In the first instance concerning the problem related to the imputation of agency where correspondence theory is employed, we know that we can now successfully bypass this issue by virtue of the notion of a recursive process. There is no problem regarding the idea of agency because we pose an idea where the operative concept is that of recursivity, not of a causal agency. Furthermore, the components subject and language are considered to be simultaneously both medium and outcome of each other; therefore, again, we are able to bypass the problem of the designation of agency. In the second instance concerning the problem of how the relationship between the individual and language might best be conceptualized, our notion of structuration provides a helpful conceptual tool. For us, subject and language are not separated concepts but rather mutually dependent components within the recursive process of structuration. This means that we do not have to think in terms of one set of elements mapping onto another set of corresponding elements or of one structure "hooking on" to another. Rather subject and language are understood to be in a duality of structure. Thus, there is no question of how one affects the other as if they were separate. There is no need, therefore, for an axis of combination—subject and language are inseparable as medium and outcome of each other.

Structuration and Sexual Difference

If we apply the concept of structuration to the issue of sexual difference I think that it could well be profitable to return to Lacan's work anew. I suggest this because of Lacan's attempt to bring the symbolic world into focus wherever psychoanalytic concerns are addressed and because sexual difference is no doubt a central area of importance in Lacanian psychoanalytic theory. A paper that Juliet Mitchell and Jacqueline Rose refer to as Lacan's "most direct exposition of the status of the phallus in the psychoanalytic account of sexuality"[30]—"The Meaning of the Phallus."[31]— would seem to be an appropriate starting point. The special relevance of this paper is that it allows us to attempt to utilize the process of language at a theoretical level by way of Lacan's use of the phallus understood as the major signifier. Speaking of the phallus as the major signifier is the means by which we gain theoretical access to the world of meaning or signification, and it is within the terms of this world that sexual difference gains its real importance from a psychoanalytic point of view.

Anatomical difference is important where sexual difference is concerned but not "in itself." What is important from a psychoanalytic point of view is the meaning that is imputed to that difference and the difference that is lived out because of that meaning within the individual and his or her personal history. Note here that the giving of meaning is understood within the context of a recursive process. The subject is given and gives meaning simultaneously within the terms of the process of structuration that we now employ for theoretical explanation. How, then, are we to relate the Lacanian proposition of the phallus to our proposed concept of structuration? I do not intend to answer this question here, but it is my contention that rather than look to the structure of language in itself to theorize about sexual difference, especially 'manliness' and 'femininity', as Schneiderman has done, it is far more profitable to work with the conceptual tool of structuration and Lacan's rich and complex notion concerning the phallus:

> But simply by keeping to the function of the phallus, we can pinpoint the structure which will govern the relations between the sexes.
> Let us say that these relations will revolve around a being and a having which, because they refer to a signifier, the phallus, have the contradictory effect of on the one hand lending reality to the subject in that signifier, and on the other making unreal the relations to be signified.[32]

This is not a simple proposal concerning the division of the sexes where any type of correspondence theory or isomorphic mapping is to be employed. This proposal is one that relies on our ability to develop a theory that concerns the subject, understood as the subject in the process of structuration. By definition, this subject is understood as being un-equivocally involved in the symbolic world because together they are said to be a dual structure. How the subject becomes a sexual being within a particular linguistic world is the question that has now to be addressed. Lacan's notion of the phallus may help us in our exploration.

In the light of my consideration of Schneiderman's[33] work, what I propose is, therefore, a conceptually economical account of what is taken to involve many and varied psychological processes. To work with Lacan's concept of the phallus and the proposed tool of structuration, where subject and language are understood to form a dual structure, although conceptually economical, in no sense implies that we fail to acknowledge the nature of the complexity of the issue with which we are dealing. Rather, it is a case of Occam's razor.

The Subject in the Process of Structuration

If we employ the idea of structuration within psychoanalytic theory, applying it to the concepts of subject and language, we are in the position of having gained the conceptual tool sought to deal with the division between the concepts of subject and agency insofar as the concept of agency is redundant within this new conceptualization. In addition, although retaining those concepts that I hold are essential to the endeavor of psychoanalytic theorization, subject and language, neither is imputed with agency. This means that the impasse found in Lacan's formulations is overcome by means of a totally new type of conceptual context. This context is one of process.

It is important to recall in passing that in one of Freud's attempts to schematize the psychic apparatus we saw that there was no need for the concept of agency. This schema was based on a physiological or anatomical model of the mind and consequently assumed a basis of physiological transmissions. Therefore, subject and language which are necessarily key considerations within the present proposal are lacking in Freud's proposition. In the context under discussion, the subject is not assumed to be a physiological organism but a subject who speaks to the analyst.

Given the relevance of an application of the term *structuration* to the problem of subject and agency in psychoanalytic theory, what can we now say of the subject in psychoanalysis? Because psychoanalysis works with words, any theory of the subject must take as its focus the subject who speaks. This is certainly the emphasis of the work of Lacan; and although much richness can undoubtedly be gleaned from his formulations, it is my contention that, in part, it is because of his position concerning the agency of the letter that his theory of the subject is fraught with inconsistencies. If we start with a different contention, one in which there is no concept of agency but rather the idea of recursivity, then the subject in psychoanalysis is best understood as being *a subject within the process of structuration*. This means, in effect, that the emphasis is placed upon the process rather than upon the subject because the subject is to be understood, and can only be understood, within this precise context. Thus *we are not concerned with a theory of the subject per se* but with a theory of the subject in the process of structuration. This subject is integrally linked with language and cannot be conceptualized outside the context of the structuration process in which language is likewise essentially involved.

Is it possible, then, to provide some new schema as a way of presenting this idea of the subject in the process of structuration? Whereas Freud attempted to schematize the psychic apparatus with his topography of the id, ego, and superego, mapping these areas in a two-dimensional and spatial way, Lacan, after proposing Schema L, utilized the field of topology in his presentation of aspects of his theory of the subject. The importance of a shift from topography to topology is that rather than be bound by spatial representation, Lacan in the 1970s employed a geometry without measurement to structure the analytic experience. This means that there is no question of distance because "only the schematic network of the signifier supports the objects."[34] Can we gain from either topography or topology in an attempt to provide conceptual clarification of the proposed position? Because my proposal is that the subject be understood as the subject within a process, any attempt to schematize this notion is held to be inappropriate. The subject cannot be depicted within a three-dimensional schema, bound by space or measurement, nor would any topological figure be of help because the subject is never static and cannot be depicted as such in any type of representation. What has to be kept in mind is the idea of process. Given the context of process, the subject is understood to be in a constant state of "becoming a subject"—that is, becoming a subject in the process of structuration. Such a notion can never be pinned down by visual representation of a schematic form because there is the strong probability that any schematization will portray a static idea of what must be understood to be process.

Consequently, the subject in psychoanalysis so understood is conceptualized as neither whole nor as divided. Neither is this subject understood as an essence. The subject that is proposed here is the subject in the process of structuration with the emphasis on *in the process of structuration*. The problem then becomes not so much one of attempting to define the subject but one of endeavoring to grapple with the conceptualization of what is involved in the process of structuration itself as far as subject and language are concerned. Here, I think, we might well turn to Lacan— especially in terms of his approach to the link between language and the description of the unconscious and its processes—for he has much to say about the dependence of the subject on language, although virtually nothing to say about language and its dependence on the subject. It is not my intention to go into this here because that is a major work in itself, one that lies outside the parameters of the specific problem addressed in this book concerning agency and subject. Nevertheless, Lacan's work may well throw light on the area of psychic processes understood from the point of view of the subject-language duality.

Lacan takes language as his starting point and from that point looks to define his subject: "The question is to find a precise status for this other subject which is exactly the sort of subject that we can determine taking our point of departure in language."[35] I propose a very different point of departure. From the perspective presented in this book I propose that we take the subject/language duality as the point of departure and only then are we to look to Lacan for clarification where a linguistic conceptualization of the unconscious is concerned, keeping in mind that subject and language are now held to be medium and outcome of each other. In doing so it is important to heed D. Macey's warnings that no true theory of language emerges from Lacan's work and that the "excursion into rhetoric unwittingly demonstrates that the formations of the unconscious are structured like a discourse, but not that the unconscious is structured like a language."[36] Laplanche has also criticized Lacan on this issue on a number of occasions.[37] We need, too, to note that M. Safouan, a Lacanian analyst and theoretician, recognizes in his important paper "Female Sexuality in Psychoanalytic Doctrine,"[38] first published in 1975, that the problem of the girl's entry into the Oedipus complex is such that it demands a reformulation of the unconscious and sexuality in their relation to language. In other words, Safouan does not assume that this vitally important area of relationships has been dealt with adequately even within the Lacanian tradition where he is an eminent figure.

One avenue that would seem at this stage to be of particular relevance to my proposal, and one that may offer conceptual clarification concerning the duality of subject and language, lies in the direction of the philosophical works of Martin Heidegger. Heidegger's quest was to formulate what he termed a fundamental ontology. This means that he was interested in the meaning of Being as distinct from the beingness of beings, which is the field of metaphysics. Within the parameters of his project we find his philosophical retrieve, a research method whereby he re-collects the work of past philosophers in an attempt to discover something within them that has not yet been thought. Thus Heidegger "destroys" what he considers to be philosophically unjustifiable in the tradition and attempts to retrieve those primordial experiences from which he holds that any genuine philosophical insights flow. Among other themes,

Heidegger was always interested in the relationship between Being and language. Following his deliberations on the issue in his magnum opus *Being and Time,*[39] it is in his essay *"Logos"*[40] that he gives us his major retrieve of the philosophical foundations of the word. The latter work is particularly important in the present context because it is here that he argues that *Logos* and Being are primordially united. Furthermore he argues that the early Greeks had no word for language and that there has been an unfortunate separation of the *Logos* from its meaning as Being with a consequent inevitable domination of logic over true *Logos*-oriented, that is, Being-oriented thinking. A *Logos*-oriented emphasis takes up much of Heidegger's thought in the years to follow. In the "Letter on Humanism" of 1947, for example, he refers to thinking and language in terms of their relationship to Being:

> Thinking accomplishes the relation of Being to the essence of man. It does not make or cause the relation. Thinking brings this relation to Being solely as something handed over to it from Being. Such offering consists in the fact that in thinking Being comes to language. Language is the house of Being. In its home man dwells. Those who think and those who create with words are the guardians of this home. Their guardianship accomplishes the manifestation to language and maintains it in language through their speech.[41]

Given that the subject in structuration is interdependently linked with language and is said to be in the continual process of becoming a subject, it would seem that we could well turn to Heidegger's work for assistance in an attempt to gain conceptual clarity beyond the point at which we have now arrived.

Reference has been made in passing to Lacan's own interest in the concept of being. This was in his early years when he was taken up with Heidegger's thought. During the fifties Lacan's work is nourished by his attention to the concept of being so much so that he speaks of the analytic situation precisely in terms of this theoretical proclivity: "By *the being of the subject,* we do not mean its psychological properties, but what is hollowed out in the experience of speech, which constitutes the analytic situation."[42]

We find this leaning toward an ontological approach in reference to love, to language, and to desire. The aim of love, he tells us, is not satisfaction but being[43]; it is only in the dimension of being that the three fundamental passions—love, hate, and ignorance—can be inscribed,[44] and being only exists in the register of speech.[45] The Freudian world,

Lacan teaches, is a world of desire. "Desire is a relation of being to lack. This lack is the lack of being properly speaking."[46] By 1964 Lacan reached a point where he could speak of his earlier philosophical approach to language as only a "propaedeutic reference,"[47] and in 1972 he was distinctly hostile to the notion of being itself.[48]

Irrespective of Lacan's later neglect of a specifically ontological dimension to his theory, his earlier attention to the concept of being does indicate its potential for psychoanalytic theory construction. Given my proposal, a renewed exploration of this avenue of thought would seem to be an appropriate next step. The work of the analyst and renowned Heideggerian philosopher William Richardson represents the possibilities of a movement in this direction. His papers "Lacan and the Subject of Psychoanalysis"[49] and "Psychoanalysis and the Being-Question" can be read to support my argument.

In the former, for example, he challenges Lacan's concept of the subject. He suggests that we might explore the question of the unity of the "who" engaged in the psychoanalytic process through the concept of desire. Clearly, Richardson does not accept Lacan's subject of the unconscious as adequate for psychoanalytic experience and proposes that the question of unity cannot be easily dismissed. He puts forward the idea that we follow either or both of two paths. The first, he explains "would be to interrogate the subject in its Being—that is, as process rather than as substance or subject (*hypokeimenon*) whose task is to be (and, therefore, is in want of being), process that as such does not say I but precedes the saying and remains always capable of it."[50] The second approach "would be to explore the subject precisely in terms of its want-to-be, its primordial lack—that is, its desire."[51] Given the present argument, the first option worked out through Heidegger may well be a fruitful pursuit. In the latter paper, Richardson suggests a Heideggerian reading of Lacan and throws much light on the issue of how the unconscious can be understood as a disclosive process that is involved in "letting beings become manifest as what they are by letting them come into words."[52]

Because Heidegger took no account of the unconscious in his work, it could be thought that we have lost sight of the subject in psychoanalysis and become seduced by the subject in the everyday world. It could be argued, therefore, that an acceptance of the notion of the subject in the process of structuration into psychoanalysis leads to a failure to work with that which is specific to its field—that is, the unconscious.[53] This means that there is a danger that it may be believed that the conceptualization of the subject that I propose is one that pertains most appropriately to the social sciences.

This is particularly so given that the term *structuration,* although reconceptualized within the psychoanalytic framework, has its origins in the discourse of social theory. We have met the subject of the social sciences, or the subject of the everyday world, in the instance of the work of both Rank and Hartmann. What characterizes this subject is the underlying assumption that the subject is held to be agent of his or her thought, word, and deed. From the point of view of these theorists, the subject is said to exhibit this agency through the use of willpower. In Rank's theory, the concept of subject and the concept of will are held as a unity. In Hartmann's theory the problem of conceptualization is more complex because he inherits the inconsistencies and contradictions that have been identified in Freud's work. Although Hartmann is interested in the subject who controls action through will, he nevertheless employs many Freudian psychoanalytic concepts such as repression, the id, ego, and super-ego.

In our own case, the concept of agency and, by implication, the concept of will simply do not pertain to a structuration perspective. They are irrelevant for they are out of context. The subject proposed here, unlike the subject of the social sciences, is held to be in a recursive dual relationship with language. There is no agent within this conceptual framework, nor is there a subject who wills or determines his or her behavior. Rather, from a theoretical stance we assume a dual structure: that of subject-language, whose components can be separated for heuristic purposes alone. From a practical stance—that is, from within a clinical context—the subject is acknowledged; but the field of endeavor for the analyst is the field of language—that is, speech. It is assumed that the subject is both outcome and medium of language. This means that in the clinical context in which the subject speaks to the analyst the efficacy of will is not acknowledged, let alone recognized. Rather, the focus is upon the process of structuration, and it is from this basis that the treatment will gain its direction.

We have seen that Lacan's reading of "The Purloined Letter" is underpinned by an assumption that agency is located in the symbolic world. We have seen too how this assumption leads to inconsistencies and problems for theory construction. An alternative reading, however—one based on the assumption of the agency of the subject—produces a theoretical blind alley. This is so because it is such an assumption that underlies the notion of the subject of the everyday world: one who wills and attempts to control and who knows nothing of the effects of the unconscious. Our assumption, that of a dual structure, acknowledges the subject who speaks to the analyst, but it imputes overall dominance to neither subject nor language. Furthermore, and importantly, *it does not lose the notion of the unconscious*. Rather, an adoption of this proposal means that the idea of the unconscious, understood from the point of view of the being who speaks in the analytic situation, needs to be reconceptualized. In other words, this proposal is a radical one. An acceptance of the concept of structuration as outlined here will entail major consequences for theory construction. Its introduction necessarily involves a rethinking of the very foundations of the psychoanalytic edifice.

To be clear. It is my proposal that the concept of the subject in the process of structuration be employed at the level of a *theoretical assumption* only. This means that within the context of theory construction it is to be taken as a given and on the basis of this given other theoretical concepts are to be employed. Because the object of psychoanalysis is the unconscious, its theory must have as its prime focus the notion of the unconscious—not that of the subject. Yet, any theory of the unconscious implies some assumptions with regard to how the subject is conceptualized. Although I propose a theoretical assumption, I do not propose a theory of the subject. However, my proposal does have major implications as to how the unconscious might be conceptualized.

The Concept of the Unconscious in the Clinical Situation

What I propose, then, is that we take the subject-language duality, one that incorporates the idea of recursivity, as a theoretical assumption. Given this assumption we might now ask: How is the concept of the unconscious to be understood? Although a discussion of this formidable issue remains outside the parameters of the argument of this book, it is important to point to a possible direction, even if only for the sake of additional clarification.

It is well known that where the subject and language are considered as separate components within a theoretical framework, the problem of how the unconscious is best handled is a controversial issue. I refer, of course, to the Laplanche-Lacan debate.[54] In perhaps an oversimplified version this debate can be said to center on their respective positions with regard to the question of the primacy of language and the unconscious. From Lacan's perspective, language is the condition of the unconscious; from Laplanche's perspective, the unconscious is the condition of language. From a structuration perspective, no such problem arises. Neither language nor the unconscious is the condition of the other. Both are involved simultaneously, for as medium and outcome of one another they are said to be a dimension of the process of structuration—that is, the coming to be of the subject through speech. This coming into being through speech is to be applied to all speech, both conscious and unconscious. This is so when we do not conceptualize a split subject but rather acknowledge a double register of signifiers one of which we refer to as the basis of an unconscious discourse and unconscious memory. Thus we can say that within the clinical setting the unconscious is best understood as that which is expressed through a particular register of speech. It is that which gives rise to a non-everyday discourse and a non-conscious memory.

We saw in chapter 2 that in his second schema Freud proposed a number of inscriptions and that memory is present not once but several times over—"that it is laid down in various kinds of indications" (p. 38). We saw this point again in his 1915 query regarding whether a second registration is a change in place or a change of state: "Are we to suppose that this transcription involves a fresh record . . . Or are we rather to believe that the transposition consists in a change in the state of the idea . . . ?" (p. 64). In a much later paper, "A Note Upon the 'Mystic Writing-Pad' " (1925),[55] he explored further the idea of unconscious memory understood as a type of double inscription. Lacan, too, talks of a double inscription. In his discussion with Lemaire concerning the Laplanche-Lacan debate, he is reported to claim:

> The unconscious is purely and simply a discourse and it is as such that it necessitates the theory of the double inscription. This is proved by the fact that there may be two completely different inscriptions, although they operate on and are supported by the *same signifiers,* which simply turn their battery, their apparatus, in order to occupy topographically different places.[56]

Following both Freud and Lacan, we can think in terms of a double inscription of the signifier. However, whereas Lacan proposes that it is the signifiers that are agents, that they turn their battery, their apparatus, in order to occupy topographically different places, it is my proposal that it is the subject who positions him/herself variously and so utilizes the different registers. Thus, we can say that the subject speaks through either the conscious register—that is, utilizing one aspect of the inscription—or, alternatively, through the other register, in which case a different aspect of the inscription is utilized as well. Sometimes the subject is positioned so that only a conscious discourse is articulated. At other times, the subject, although speaking consciously, will at the same time be so positioned that s/he speaks unconsciously as well. What is crucial here is the positioning of the subject who speaks.

Rather than refer to the subject of the conscious or the subject of the unconscious, our assumption allows us to refer to the subject who positions him/herself differentially so that at times s/he speaks via the conscious register alone and at other time through both registers simultaneously. It is the analyst's work to recognize when the subject is positioned so that s/he articulates through the latter. The interest of clinical psychoanalysis is in that aspect of the subject's being that is particular to the unconscious. It does not directly concern itself with those moments when the subject who speaks to the analyst is positioned so that the words spoken, although an articulation and expression of one aspect of his/her coming to be, pertain to the arena of a conscious discourse and conscious memory. That the analyst hears this unconscious articulation means, from our point of view, that there is the possibility that the subject's process of coming into being be enhanced.

From a structuration perspective, the clinical context is unique. It and it alone, provides the means, through the work of the analyst, by which the subject can hear him/herself speak unconsciously: that is, when so positioned that the unconscious discourse is expressive of a dimension of being that elsewhere must necessarily remain unheard. Although the fullness of being can never be achieved, for the subject is involved in a process that only death will conclude, the work of analysis is a work whereby the subject's potential to come into being is maximized. No other path is comparable.

These issues among many others require soundly constructed theoretical explication. All that is possible here is to point to implications and possible avenues for thought if one is to accept the proposal made. One final point is necessary before concluding. I return now to an issue that has occupied much of our attention: the psychic apparatus.

The Subject and the Psychic Apparatus

In the earlier chapters of this book we saw that Freud provided a schema of the psychic apparatus that remained disconnected from the notion of the subject. Consequently his theory, and the theory of those who un- questioningly adopt his schema, is limited to what can be achieved by means of the explication of these concepts *in and by themselves*. For example, Hartmann elaborated further on the concept of the ego, and Klein elaborated upon the concept of the id with major structural changes being suggested. But both these theorists are limited by the nature of the unacknowledged assumptions made. In other words for these two theo- rists it is the *apparatus* that is the focal point of theorization, not the subject. In this sense both Hartmann and Klein are Freudian because— like Freud before them—they, too, deliberate upon the psychic apparatus rather than upon the subject in psychoanalysis. Both develop their theory from the structural basis of Freud's threefold schema, but neither looks to the nature of the subject. This means that any undertaking of psychoana- lytic theorization within the Freudian tradition can do little more than "fiddle" with the apparatus while simultaneously ignoring questions that demand radical interrogation: How is the subject in psychoanalysis to be conceptualized? What is the nature of agency where this subject is con- cerned? Only when these questions have been addressed can psychoana- lytic theory postulate mechanisms, processes, and structures that are in line with those assumptions underpinning them. Failure to address these questions means that psychoanalytic theory can hope to do little more than provide the clothing for an emperor who remains unknown.

The work of Jacques Lacan, however, is of particular importance in regard to this issue. Lacan claims to be Freudian, but perhaps it is more appropriate in the present context to say that Lacan is Lacanian in that he does not fall into the category of those theoreticians who work in the domain of the apparatus alone. He is always and passionately concerned with the question of the subject. In answering these questions Lacan draws upon numerous academic domains, in particular linguistics, but bases his answer on a deterministic argument that has been found to be irreconcilable with his own theoretical postulations. Nevertheless Lacan is important here because he takes as his starting point the theory of the subject and proceeds to theorize about the nature of the psychic apparatus in the light of his fundamental tenets. I want to look briefly at this point because it will exemplify what I think has yet to be dealt with given my proposal of the subject in structuration. Because the subject in psychoanalysis is characterized by both speech and the unconscious, as was the *hystérique d'occasion,* there is still need to conceptualize the idea of the psychic apparatus within the context of the structuration—that is, if we wish to remain within the Freudian tradition.

Ragland-Sullivan explains that Lacan recast Freud's second topology. He has collapsed the id and ego into the *moi* and extended the id into the realm of unconscious desire. The super-ego, conceptualized on the basis of the split subject, becomes for Lacan "the structural mechanism by which the identificatory *moi* is repressed as an ideal ego and the social *je* formed, and thus part of both subjects."[57] The super-ego is formed when the child separates psychically from the mother at the end of the mirror stage. Similarly, Lacan has reformulated the concept of repression in the light of his underpinning theory of the subject in psychoanalysis. In his theory, primary repression is formulated in terms of "the fixing of a primary, signifying chain in the pre-specular and mirror-stage periods."[58] This means that for him neither sexuality nor emotion is repressed, but the earliest representations of desire in their link to the (m)other. Notice how this reformulation is derived from and is seen in the light of his theory of the split subject as presented earlier. Secondary repression, then, "concerns the desire that coincides with the end of the mirror stage."[59] It is this repression that, for Lacan, creates the unconscious barrier between consciousness and perception and brings about the misrecognition of truth. It arises from the division of the psyche by language whereby there is a subject of speech and a subject of identification. Because Lacan has questioned the nature of the subject, he is in a position to theorize about processes and structures in the light of his stance concerning the subject in psychoanalysis.

Just as Lacan has reformulated the apparatus in the light of his notion of the split subject, so, too, is reformulation necessary in the light of the proposal of the subject in the process of structuration. This project is, of course, beyond the scope of the present argument, but there is now need for further work in the area of reconceptualizing psychoanalytic concepts in general on the basis of an underpinning dual structure.

Conclusion

At the outset of this investigation I posed the question of how the notions of agency and subject are understood at a theoretical level within the framework of psychoanalysis. As a means of answering the question I turned to Freud, Hartmann, Klein, and Lacan. In the face of the problems that I have shown to be the consequence of adherence to a separation between the concepts of subject and agency within the core of psychoanalytic theory, I have proposed that the concept of structuration be introduced within the field of theory construction. The introduction of this notion provides us with a conceptual tool that is able, first, to overcome the need for the use of the concept of agency altogether and, second, to eradicate a conceptual separation between subject and language while maintaining both in a duality of structure.

Thus, it is my proposal that psychoanalytic theory need not be hampered by the problem of agency and that the subject in psychoanalysis is most productively conceptualized in terms of the subject in the process of structuration. As a means of working with the newly introduced conceptual tool of structuration within the field of psychoanalysis I have suggested that we turn anew to the work of Lacan and Heidegger. In each case clarification and elaboration of some aspects of the process of structuration may be gained and, in the light of the findings of this further work, the idea of the unconscious might well be retheorized.

Finally, given the proposal made in this book, I think we are now in a position to claim that Humpty Dumpty asked the wrong question.

Notes

Introduction

1. D. Hume, *Treatise on Human Nature* (Oxford: Claredon Press, 1928), 252.

2. See P. Marshall Jones, *French Introspectives: From Montaigne to André Gide* (London: Cambridge University Press, 1937).

3. V. E. Frankl, *Man's Search for Meaning: An Introduction to Logotherapy,* trans. I. Lasch (London: Hodder & Stoughton, 1964).

4. For example: G. H. Mead, *Mind, Self and Soceity: From the Standpoint of a Social Behaviourist,* ed. C. W. Morris (Chicago: University of Chicago Press, 1962).

5. For example: A. Schutz, *The Phenomenology of the Social World,* trans. G. Walsh and F. Lehnert (London: Heinemann, 1972); A. Schutz and T. Luckmann, *The Structures of the Life-World,* trans. R. M. Zaner and H. T. Englehardt, Jr. (London: Heinemann, 1974).

6. Unless otherwise stated all references to the works of S. Freud are taken from *The Standard Edition of the Complete Psychological Works of Sigmund Freud,* trans. and ed. J. Strachey (London: Hogarth Press and Institute of Psycho-Analysis, 1953–74), hereafter cited as *S.E.*

7. T. S. Eliot, *Four Quartets* (London: Faber and Faber, 1979), 47.

8. See: J. Sturrock, ed., *Structuralism and Since* (Oxford: Oxford University Press, 1979), 4; J. Mitchell and J. Rose, eds., *Jacques Lacan and the école freudienne: Feminine Sexuality* (London: Macmillan, 1982), 4; D. Macey, *Lacan in Contexts* (London: Verso, 1988), 44–74 for a very interesting argument that Lacan was not only influenced by surrealism but that his writing is part of the same web.

9. J. Lacan, *Écrits: A Selection,* trans. A. Sheridan (London: Tavistock, 1977).

10. J. Lacan (1953–54), *The Seminar of Jacques Lacan. Book I. Freud's Papers*

on Technique 1953–1954, trans. J. Forrester, ed. J-A Miller (Cambridge: Cambridge University Press, 1988).

11. J. Lacan (1954–55), *The Seminar of Jacques Lacan. Book II. The Ego in Freud's Theory and in the Technique of Psychoanalysis 1954–1955,* trans. S. Tomaselli, ed. J-A. Miller (Cambridge: Cambridge University Press, 1988).

12. J. Lacan (1964), *The Four Fundamental Concepts of Psycho-Analysis,* trans. A. Sheridan, ed. J-A. Miller (Harmondsworth: Penguin, 1979).

13. B. Bettleheim, *Freud and Man's Soul* (New York: Alfred A. Knopf, 1983).

14. Ibid., 4.

15. Ibid., 77.

16. See F. J. Sulloway, *Freud, Biologist of the Mind: Beyond the Psychoanalytic Legend* (New York: Basic Books, 1979), 365.

1. Subject and Agent

1. S. Freud (1914), "On the History of the Psycho-Analytic Movement', *S.E.* 14: 7–66.

2. S. Freud (1925 [1924]), *An Autobiographical Study, S.E.* 20: 7–74.

3. S. Freud (1892–93), "A Case of Successful Treatment by Hypnotism With Some Remarks on the Origin of Hysterical Symptoms Through 'Counter-Will,' " *S.E.* 1: 117–28.

4. Ibid., 117.

5. Ibid., 117.

6. Ibid., 119.

7. Ibid., 120.

8. Ibid., 120.

9. Ibid., 121.

10. Ibid., 122.

11. Ibid., 123.

12. Ibid., 123, emphasis in the original.

13. Ibid., 124.

14. S. Freud (1893–95), "Case 2: Frau Emmy von N., Age 40, from Livonia," *S.E.* 2: 48–105.

15. S. Freud (1892–93), "A Case of Successful Treatment by Hypnotism," *S.E.* 1: 124, emphasis in the original.

16. J. Breuer (1893–95), *Studies on Hysteria, S.E.* 2: 216.

17. J. Breuer and S. Freud (1893–95), *Studies on Hysteria, S.E.* 2.

18. S. Freud (1896), "The Aetiology of Hysteria," *S.E.* 3: 191–221.

19. Breuer, *Studies on Hysteria,* 216.

20. Ibid., 214.

21. S. Freud (1894), "The Neuro-Psychoses of Defense," *S.E.* 3: 45–61.

22. Breuer, *Studies on Hysteria,* 214.

23. Freud (1893–95), *Studies on Hysteria,* 286.

24. J. Breuer and S. Freud (1893), "Preliminary Communication," *S.E.* 2: 10.

25. S. Freud (1893–95), "The Psychotherapy of Hysteria," *S.E.* 2: 253–305.
26. Ibid., 269.
27. Ibid., 269–70.
28. Strachey (1955), *S.E.* 2: 10n.
29. S. Freud (1894), "The Neuro-Psychoses of Defense," *S.E.* 3: 46–47, emphasis in the original.
30. Ibid., 52–53.
31. Ibid., 47.
32. S. Freud (1896), "Further Remarks on the Neuro-Psychoses of Defense," *S.E.* 3: 163–85.
33. Ibid., 162, emphasis in the original.
34. S. Freud (1896), "The Aetiology of Neuroses," *S.E.* 3: 211, emphasis in the original.
35. S. Freud (1899), "Screen Memories," *S.E.* 3: 303–22.
36. S. Freud (1915–16), *Introductory Lectures on Psycho-Analysis, S.E.* 15: 97–98.

2. The Freud-Fliess Correspondence

1. Cited in J. Masson, trans. and ed., *The Complete Letters of Sigmund Freud to Wilhelm Fliess 1887–1904* (Cambridge: Harvard University Press, 1985), 11–12.
2. See J. Malcolm, *In the Freud Archives* (London: Flamingo, 1986), for a description of the politics and background involved.
3. For the use Masson has made of this new primary-source material see J. J. Masson, *The Assault on Truth: Freud's Suppression of the Seduction Theory* (New York: Farrar, Straus & Giroux, 1984).
4. For a discussion of the importance of this point see F. M. Moran, "The Anti-Freud Genre," *The Age Monthly Review,* 7 July 1987 (3), 10–11.
5. Masson, *The Complete Letters,* 12.
6. Freud, *The Complete Letters,* 127.
7. Ibid., 129.
8. Ibid., 141.
9. Ibid., 150.
10. Ibid. (1896), 159.
11. R. Wollheim, *Freud* (London: Fontana, 1971), 52.
12. S. Freud (1895), "Project for a Scientific Psychology," *S.E.* 1: 302.
13. Ibid., 323.
14. Ibid., 327.
15. Ibid., 328, emphasis in the original.
16. Ibid., 322, emphasis in the original.
17. See S. Freud (1901), *The Psychopathology of Everyday Life, S.E.* 6: 154, 158n., 234, 259, 275–76.
18. Freud (1895), "Project," *S.E.* 1: 317, emphasis in the original.

19. Ibid., 358.
20. Strachey (1966), *S.E.* 1: 292.
21. Ibid., 290n. His introduction to *S.E.* 4 is also excellent as far as the "Project" is concerned.
22. Ibid., 293.
23. J. Laplanche, *Life and Death in Psychoanalysis,* trans. and introd. J. Mehlman (Baltimore: Johns Hopkins University Press, 1976), 66.
24. Freud, *The Complete Letters,* 164.
25. Ibid., 188.
26. Ibid., 207.
27. Ibid., 207–8, emphasis in the original.
28. Ibid., 208.
29. Freud later developed an ultimate-level explanation of the repression of sexual instincts. See Sulloway, *Freud, Biologist of the Mind,* esp. 369.
30. See Masson, *The Complete Letters,* 459.

3. The First Topography

1. Masson, *The Complete Letters,* 303.
2. Ibid. (1897), 278.
3. E. Jones, *The Life and Work of Sigmund Freud* (Harmondsworth: Penguin, 1964), 306.
4. S. Freud (1900), *The Interpretation of Dreams, S.E.* 5: 536, emphasis in the original.
5. Ibid., 536.
6. Ibid., 538.
7. Ibid., 540.
8. Ibid., 541.
9. Ibid., 588.
10. In 1919 Freud added a footnote as follows: "If we attempted to proceed further with this schematic picture, in which the systems are set out in linear succession, we should have to reckon with the fact that the system next beyond the Pcs. is the one to which consciousness must be ascribed—in other words, that Pcpt. = Cs" (*S.E.* 5: 541). This does not clarify anything, rather it indicates a problem that Freud is having with his attempt to conceptualize the psyche. Here he confuses the structure (topography) with the function of the apparatus.
11. Ibid., 540.
12. Ibid., 542.
13. Freud, *The Interpretation of Dreams, S.E.* 4: 144.
14. Ibid., 145.
15. Ibid., 567.
16. Freud (1933[1932]), *New Introductory Lectures on Psycho-Analysis, S.E.* 22: 72.

17. Freud (1900), *The Interpretation of Dreams,* S.E. 5: 600, emphasis in the original.

18. Ibid., 588.

19. Ibid., 603.

20. Ibid., 612–13.

21. Ibid., 604, emphasis in the original.

22. Ibid., 605.

23. Freud (1900), *The Interpretation of Dreams,* S.E. 4: 267.

24. Ibid., 234, emphasis in the original.

25. Freud (1919), *The Interpretation of Dreams,* S.E. 5: 580–81n.

26. Ibid., 557.

27. Ibid., 557.

28. Ibid., 557.

29. Ibid., 558.

30. Ibid., 558.

31. Ibid., 558.

32. Ibid., 610.

33. Ibid., 610.

34. Strachey (1953), *S.E.* 4: xviii.

35. Freud (1916–17), *Introductory Lectures,* S.E. 16: 389.

4. *The Metapsychology*

1. S Freud (1905), *Three Essays on the Theory of Sexuality,* S.E. 7: 123–243.

2. S. Freud (1905 [1901]), "Fragment of an Analysis of a Case of Hysteria," *S.E.* 7: 1–122.

3. S. Freud (1909), "Analysis of a Phobia in a Five-Year-Old-Boy," *S.E.* 10: 1–149.

4. S. Freud (1909), "Notes upon a Case of Obsessional Neurosis," *S.E.* 10: 155–318.

5. S. Freud (1913 [1912–13]), *Totem and Taboo,* S.E. 13: 1–161.

6. S. Freud (1911–1915 [1914]), "Papers on Technique," *S.E.* 12: 85–171.

7. S. Freud (1911), "Two Principles of Mental Functioning," *S.E.* 12: 223.

8. Ibid., 224.

9. Freud in Jones, *The Life and Work,* 429.

10. H. Abraham and E. Freud, eds., and B. Marsh and H. Abraham, trans., *A Psycho-Analytic Dialogue: The Letters of Sigmund Freud & Karl Abraham 1907–1926* (New York: Basic Books, 1965), 213.

11. Jones, *The Life and Work,* 435.

12. S. Freud (1915), "Instincts and Their Vicissitudes", *S.E.* 14: 121–22, emphasis in the original.

13. S. Freud (1910), "The Psycho-Analytic View of Psychogenic Disturbance of Vision," *S.E.* 11: 209–18.

14. Freud, "Instincts and Their Vicissitudes," 124.

15. Ibid., 124.

16. Ibid., 124.

17. Ibid., 138.

18. Ibid., 137, emphasis in the original.

19. S. Freud (1940 [1938]), *An Outline of Psycho-Analysis,* S.E. 23: 148.

20. Freud, "On the History," *S.E.,* 16.

21. Freud, *An Autobiographical Study,* 30.

22. S. Freud (1910 [1909]), *Five Lectures on Psycho-Analysis,* S.E. 11: 24.

23. Freud, "Notes upon a Case," 196.

24. Bettleheim, *Freud and Man's Soul,* 93.

25. Ibid., 93.

26. S. Freud (1915), "Repression," *S.E.* 14: 147.

27. Ibid., 148.

28. Ibid., 153.

29. Ibid., 154, emphasis in the original.

30. Ibid., 148.

31. Ibid., 149.

32. Ibid., 153.

33. S. Freud (1912), "A Note on the Unconscious in Psycho-Analysis," *S.E.* 12: 260–66.

34. Freud (1915), "The Unconscious," *S.E.* 14: 166.

35. Ibid., 175, emphasis in the original.

36. Ibid., 175.

37. Ibid., 176.

38. Ibid., 183.

39. Ibid., 190.

40. Ibid., 193.

41. For an excellent work on this topic of Freud and language see J. Forrester, *Language and the Origins of Psychoanalysis* (London: Macmillan, 1980).

42. S. Freud, *Zur Auffassung der Aphasien* (Vienna: 1891), trans. *On Aphasia* (London and New York: 1953).

43. Freud, "The Unconscious," 202.

44. Ibid., 202–3.

45. Ibid., 202.

46. See chapter 2 of *The Ego and the Id, S.E.* 19. For earlier references see S.E. 1:111; 5: 617, 574; 12: 213–36.

47. F. de Saussure (1915), *Cours de linguistique générale* (Paris: Payot, 1967).

48. Freud (1922), *S.E.* 19: 283–84.

49. Freud (1917[1915]), "A Metapsychological Supplement to the Theory of Dreams," *S.E.* 14: 233, emphasis in the original.

50. Freud (1914), "On Narcissism: An Introduction" *S.E.* 14: 94.

51. Ibid., 95.

52. Freud (1917[1915]), "Mourning and Melancholia," *S.E.* 14: 247.

53. Ibid., 249.

5. *The Second Topography*

1. S. Freud (1920), *Beyond the Pleasure Principle, S.E.* 28: 7–64.

2. Ibid., 19–20, emphasis in the original.

3. S. Freud (1921), *Group Psychology and the Analysis of the Ego, S.E.* 28: 67–143.

4. S. Freud (1923), *The Ego and the Id, S.E.* 19: 3–66.

5. See Jones, *The Life and Work,* 545. This paper was never published.

6. Freud (1923), cited in Jones, *The Life and Work,* 557.

7. Freud, *The Ego and the Id,* 24.

8. S. Freud (1933[1932]), *New Introductory Lectures on Psycho-Analysis, S.E.* 22: 7–182.

9. Freud, *The Ego and the Id,* 17.

10. Ibid., 25.

11. Ibid., 25.

12. Ibid., 36.

13. Ibid., 36.

14. Ibid., 53.

15. Ibid., 55.

16. Ibid., 56.

17. Ibid., 56.

18. Bettleheim, *Freud and Man's Soul,* 55.

19. Ibid., 61.

20. Ibid., 55.

21. Ibid., 57.

22. Ibid., 58.

23. S. Freud (1926[1925]), *Inhibitions, Symptoms and Anxiety, S.E.* 20: 87–172.

24. Ibid., 89, emphasis in the original.

25. Ibid., 95.

26. S. Freud (1930[1929]), *Civilization and Its Discontents, S.E.* 21: 60–61.

27. Freud cited in Jones, *The Life and Work,* 613.

28. Freud (1933[1932]), "The Dissection of the Psychical Personality," *S.E.* 22: 57.

29. Ibid., 58.

30. S. Freud (1940[1938]), "Splitting of the Ego in the Process of Defense," *S.E.* 23: 275–78.

31. Ibid., 79.

32. O. Rank, *Beyond Psychology* (New York: Dover, 1941), 34.

33. Ibid., 34.

34. Ibid., 48.

35. Ibid., 50, emphasis my own.

6. A Problem Concerning the Subject

1. A. Freud, *Einführung in die Technik der Kinderanalyse* (Leipzig: Internationaler Psychoanalytischer Verlag, 1927).

2. A. Freud, *The Ego and the Mechanisms of Defense* (London: Hogarth Press and Institute of Psycho-Analysis, 1937).

3. A. Freud, *The Writings of Anna Freud*, vols. 1–8 (New York: International Universities Press, 1966–80).

4. A. Freud, *The Ego and the Mechanisms of Defense*, 4.

5. Ibid., 58.

6. Ibid., 100.

7. Ibid., 102.

8. See E. Young-Bruehl, *Anna Freud* (London: Macmillan, 1988).

9. R. Lowenstein, *International Journal of Psycho-Analysis* (1970), 51: 419.

10. H. Hartmann (1938), *Ego Psychology and the Problem of Adaptation*, trans. D. Rapaport (New York: International Universities Press, 1958).

11. H. Hartmann, *Essays on Ego Psychology: Selected Problems in Psychoanalytic Theory* (London: Hogarth Press and Institute of Psycho-Analysis, 1964).

12. Hartmann, *Ego Psychology*, 4, emphasis in the original.

13. Freud, "On the History," 50.

14. S. Freud (1916–17[1915–17]), "The Common Neurotic State," *S.E.* 16: 379.

15. Hartmann, *Ego Psychology*, 8–9, emphasis in the original.

16. Ibid., 11.

17. Ibid., 11.

18. Ibid., 15.

19. Ibid., 74.

20. Ibid., 75.

21. Hartmann (1947), "On Rational and Irrational Action" in *Essays*, 39.

22. Ibid., 92.

23. Ibid., 67.

24. Hartmann (1950), "Comments on the Psychoanalytic Theory of the Ego," in *Essays*, 114.

25. Hartmann, *Ego Psychology*, 22, emphasis in the original.

26. Ibid., 24.

27. Ibid., 51, emphasis in the original.

28. Hartmann (1956), "Notes on the Reality Principle," in *Essays*, 244.

29. Ibid., 257.

30. Ibid., 257.

31. Ibid., 257.

32. See A. Schutz, *Collected Papers I: The Problem of Social Reality*, ed. M. Natanson (The Hague: Martinus Nijoff, 1962); *On Phenomenology and Social Relations: Selected Writings*, ed. H. Wagner (Chicago: University of Chicago Press,

1970); *The Phenomeonology of the Social World,* trans. G. Walsh and F. Lehert (London: Heinemann, 1972).

33. See A. Schutz and T. Luckmann, *The Structure of the Life-World,* trans. R. Zaner and H. Engelhardt, Jr. (London: Heinemann, 1974).

34. Hartmann, *Ego Psychology,* 3.

35. Ibid., 3.

36. Hartmann (1939), "Psycho-analysis and the Concept of Health," in *Essays,* 3–18.

37. Hartmann, "Psychoanalysis and Sociology" 308–21.

38. For a discussion of phenomenological philosophy and sociology see M. Phillipson, "Phenomenological Philosophy and Sociology," in *New Directions in Sociological Theory,* P. Filmer, M. Phillipson, D. Silverman, and D. Walsh (London: Collier, 1972), 119–63.

39. Hartmann, "Psychoanalysis and the Concept of Health," 8.

40. Ibid., 15.

41. Hartmann, *Ego Psychology,* 20.

42. Ibid., 21.

43. Hartmann, "Psychoanalysis and Sociology," in *Essays,* 21.

44. Ibid., 29.

45. P. Grosskurth, *Melanie Klein: Her World and Her Work* (London: Hodder & Stoughton, 1986), 68.

46. Ibid., 91.

47. M. Klein (1921), "The Development of a Child," in *The Writings of Melanie Klein,* ed. R. Money-Kyrle, vol. 1 (London: Hogarth Press and Institute of Psycho-Analysis, 1975), 1–53, hereafter cited as *W. M. K.*

48. Ibid., 22.

49. Ibid., 1–2.

50. M. Klein (1923), "The Role of the School in the Libidinal Development of the Child", *W.M.K.* 1: 72.

51. M. Klein (1923), "Early Analysis," *W. M. K.* 1: 77–105.

52. Ibid., 83–84.

53. M. Klein (1946), "Notes on Some Schizoid Mechanisms," *W. M. K.* 3: 11–12.

54. M. Klein (1958), "On the Development of Mental Functioning," *W. M. K.* 3: 243.

55. M. Klein (1959), "Our Adult World and Its Roots in Infancy," *W. M. K.* 3: 249, emphasis in the original.

56. M. Klein (1929), "Personification in the Play of Children," *W. M. K.* 1: 200.

57. M. Klein, "On the Development," 245.

58. Ibid., 243.

59. Ibid., 245.

60. Ibid., 240.

61. Ibid., 243.

62. M. Klein (1928), "Early Stages of the Oedipus Conflict," *W. M. K.* 1: 187.

63. Klein, "Personification in the Play," *W. M. K.* 1: 204.

64. M. Klein (1931), "A Contribution to the Theory of Intellectual Inhibition," *W. M. K.* 1: 243.

65. M. Klein (1932), "The Psycho-Analysis of Children," *W. M. K.* 2.

66. Ibid., 148.

67. Ibid., 151.

68. Ibid., 153.

69. Ibid., 199.

70. Ibid., 199.

71. Ibid., 206–7.

72. Ibid., 206n.

73. Ibid., 222.

74. Ibid., 277.

75. Ibid., 249.

76. M. Klein (1935), "A Contribution to the Psychogenesis of Manic-Depressive States," *W. M. K.* 1: 262.

77. Ibid., 264.

78. Ibid., 265.

79. Ibid., 287.

80. M. Klein (1940), "Mourning and Its Relation to Manic-Depressive States," *W. M. K.* 1: 362.

81. M. Klein (1946), "Notes on Some Schizoid Mechanisms," *W. M. K.* 3: 5–6.

82. M. Klein (1952), "Some Theoretical Conclusions Regarding the Emotional Life of the Infant," *W. M. K.* 3: 62.

83. Ibid., 63.

84. Klein (1958), "On the Development," 246.

85. Ibid., 238.

86. Ibid., 241.

7. A Problem Concerning Agency

1. J. Lacan (1956), "Seminar on 'The Purloined Letter,' " *Yale French Studies* (1972), 48–50: 38–72.

2. D. Funt, "The Question of the Subject: Lacan and Psychoanalysis," *Psychoanalytic Review* (1973), 60 (3): 393.

3. S. Leclaire and Lacan, *The Seminar of Jacques Lacan. Book II: The Ego in Freud's Theory and in the Technique of Psychoanalysis 1954–1955,* trans. S. Tomaselli, ed. J. A. Miller (Cambridge: Cambridge University Press, 1988), 55.

4. S. Leclaire, in *Seminar II,* 62.

5. J. Lacan (1960), "The Subversion of the Subject and the Dialectic of

Desire in the Freudian Unconscious', in *Écrits: A Selection*, trans. A. Sheridan (London: Tavistock, 1977), 313.

6. See E. Ragland-Sullivan, *Jacques Lacan and the Philosophy of Psychoanalysis* (London: Croom Helm, 1986), 28, for an interesting point concerning the problem of publication dates.

7. J. Lacan (1949), "The Mirror Stage as Formative of the Function of the I as Revealed in Psychoanalytic Experience," in *Écrits*, 4.

8. Ibid., 6–7, emphasis in the original.

9. J. Lacan (1958), "The Signification of the Phallus," in *Écrits*, 287.

10. Lacan formulated and reformulated the concept of desire. Ragland-Sullivan points out that in 1936 Lacan was interested in a Hegelian phenomenology of desire, whereas in 1947 it was the dialectical scope of desire that concerned him. In 1958 he continued to develop a Hegelian thesis/antithesis/synthesis model but in the realm of the Real (see *Jacques Lacan and the Philosophy of Psychoanalysis*, 74–75).

11. J. Lacan (1966), "Of Structure as an Inmixing of an Otherness Prerequisite to Any Subject Whatever," in *The Languages of Criticism and the Sciences of Man*, ed. R. Macksey and E. Donato (Baltimore: Johns Hopkins, 1970), 191.

12. Lacan, *Seminar II*, 58.

13. Ibid., 57.

14. Ibid., 59.

15. Ibid., 159.

16. Ibid., 52.

17. Lacan, "The Subversion of the Subject," 298.

18. Ibid., 299.

19. Lacan (1957), "The Agency of the Letter in the Unconscious or Reason Since Freud," in *Écrits*, 166.

20. Lacan, *The Seminar of Jacques Lacan. Book II. The Ego in Freud's Theory and in the Technique of Psychoanalysis 1954–1955*, trans. S. Tomaselli, ed. J. A. Miller (Cambridge: Cambridge University Press, 1988).

21. It also appears in the text "On the Possible Treatment of Psychosis," in *Écrits*, 193.

22. Lacan, *Seminar II*, 243.

23. Ibid., 244.

24. Ibid., 246.

25. J. Lacan (1953), "The function and Field of Speech and Language in Psychoanalysis," in *Écrits*, 90.

26. Ibid., 90.

27. Lacan, "Of Structure," 192.

28. Ibid., 192.

29. Ibid., 193.

30. Ibid., 194.

31. J. Lacan (1975), "Geneva Lecture on the Symptom," *Analysis* 1 (1989): 13.

32. E. Bär (1971), "The Language of the Unconscious According to Jacques Lacan," *Semiotica* 3: 241–68.

33. A. Lemaire, *Jacques Lacan*, trans. D. Macey (London: Routledge and Kegan Paul, 1970), 161.

34. Ragland-Sullivan, *Jacques Lacan*, 1.

35. Ibid., 62.

36. Ibid., 60.

37. Ibid., 43.

38. Ibid., 22.

39. Freud, *The Interpretation of Dreams*, 58n.

40. Lacan, *Seminar II*, 283.

41. Lacan, *Ibid.*, 191–205; *Yale French Studies* (1972), 48–50: 38–72; *Écrits* (Paris: Editions du Seuil, 1966), 11–61.

42. Lacan, "Seminar on 'The Purloined Letter,' " 40.

43. E. A. Poe (1845), "The Purloined Letter," in *Edgar Allan Poe: Selected Writings*, ed. D. Galloway (Harmondsworth: Penguin, 1967), 332–49.

44. Ibid., 332.

45. Ibid.

46. Ibid., 333.

47. Lacan, *Seminar II*, 196.

48. Lacan, "Seminar on 'The Purloined Letter,' " 60.

49. J. Lacan (1964), *The Four Fundamental Concepts of Psycho-Analysis*, trans. A. Sheridan, ed. J. -A. Miller (Harmondsworth: Penguin, 1979), 67.

50. Ibid., 207.

51. Lacan, *Seminar II*, 99.

52. Lacan, *The Four Fundamental Concepts*, 250–51.

53. Ibid., 126.

54. Lacan, *Seminar I*, 125, emphasis in the original.

55. Lacan, *The Four Fundamental Concepts*, 67.

56. See *Écrits: A Selection*, 313; *Four Fundamental Concepts*, 218.

57. Lacan, "The Signification of the Phallus," 284, emphasis in the original.

58. Lacan, *The Four Fundamental Concepts*, 157.

59. Ibid., 157.

60. Lacan, *Seminar I*, 266.

61. Lacan, *Seminar II*, 171.

62. Ibid., 175, emphasis in the original.

63. Ibid., 293.

64. Ibid., 292, emphasis in the original.

65. Lacan, *Seminar I*, 157.

66. Ibid., 74.

67. Ibid., 271.

68. S. Žižek, *The Sublime Object of Ideology* (London and New York: Verso, 1989).

69. Ibid. 46.

70. Ibid., 178.

71. Ibid., 180.
72. Ibid., 175.
73. Ibid., emphasis in the original.
74. S. Freud (1905), "Psychical (or Mental) Treatment," *S. E. 7:* 283.
75. L. Carroll, *Through the Looking-Glass and What Alice Found There* (London: Macmillan, 1948), 114, emphasis in the original.

8. A Conceptual Tool of Structuration

1. Lacan, *The Four Fundamental Concepts,* 18, emphasis in the original.
2. A. Giddens, *Capitalism and Modern Social Theory: An Analysis of the Writings of Marx, Durkheim and Max Weber* (Cambridge: Cambridge University Press, 1971). A. Giddens, *The Class Structure of the Advanced Societies* (London: Hutchinson, 1973).

A. Giddens, *New Rules of Sociological Method: A Positive Critique of Interpretative Sociologies* (London: Hutchinson, 1976).

A. Giddens, *Central Problems in Social Theory: Action, Structure and Contradiction in Social Analysis* (London: Macmillan, 1979).

A. Giddens, *Social Theory and Modern Sociology* (Cambridge, United Kingdom: Polity Press, 1987).

3. Giddens, *Central Problems,* 69–70, emphasis in the original.
4. M. Archer, *Culture and Agency. The Place of Culture in Social Theory* (Cambridge: Cambridge University Press, 1988).
5. S. Schneiderman, *Returning to Freud. Clinical Psychoanalysis in the School of Lacan* (New Haven: Yale University Press, 1980).

S. Schneiderman, *Jacques Lacan: The Death of an Intellectual Hero* (Cambridge: Harvard University Press, 1983).

S. Schneiderman, *Rat Man* (New York: New York University Press, 1986).

6. S. Schneiderman, *An Angel Passes: How the Sexes Became Undivided* (New York: New York University Press, 1988).
7. Schneiderman, *An Angel Passes,* 14.
8. Ibid., 12.
9. Ibid., 13.
10. Ibid., 13.
11. Ibid., 165.
12. Ibid., 165.
13. Ibid., 263.
14. Ibid., 274.
15. Ibid., 261, emphasis my own.
16. Ibid., 271–2.
17. Ibid., 290.
18. Ibid., 279.
19. Ibid., 290.
20. Ibid., 295.

21. Ibid., 310.

22. Ibid., 292.

23. Ibid., 313.

24. Ibid., 313.

25. Ibid., 330, emphasis in the original.

26. Ibid., 331.

27. Ibid., 331.

28. Ibid., 14.

29. Ibid., 29, emphasis my own.

30. Mitchell and Rose, eds., *Feminine Sexuality*, 74.

31. J. Lacan (1958), "The Meaning of the Phallus" in *Feminine Sexuality*, ed. J. Mitchell and J. Rose, 74–85. This paper is also published in *Écrits: A Selection* as "The Signification of the Phallus."

32. Lacan in *Feminine Sexuality*, 83–84.

33. For Schneiderman's response to my criticism of his thesis see "Response to Frances Moran," *Analysis* 2 (1990): 91–96.

34. J. A. Miller, "Elements of Epistemology," *Analysis* 1 (1989): 30.

35. Lacan, "Of Structure as an Inmixing," 189.

36. D. Macey, *Lacan in Contexts* (London: Verso, 1988), 175.

37. See, for example, J. Laplanche, *New Foundations for Psychoanalysis* (Oxford: Basil Blackwell, 1989), 41.

38. M. Safouan (1975), "Female Sexuality in Psychoanalytic Doctrine," in *Feminine Sexuality*, 123–36.

39. M. Heidegger, *Being and Time,* trans. J. Macquarrie and E. Robinson (New York: Harper & Row, 1962), 55–58.

40. M. Heidegger (1944), "Logos" (Heraclitus, Fragment 850) in *Early Greek Thinking,* trans. D. Krell and F. Capuzzi (New York: Harper & Row, 1975), 59–78.

41. M. Heidegger (1947), "Letter on Humanism," trans. F. A. Capuzzi and J. Gray in *Basic Writings from Being and Time (1927) to The Task of Thinking (1964),* ed. D. Krell (New York: Harper & Row, 1977), 193.

42. Lacan, *Seminar I,* 230.

43. Ibid., 276.

44. Ibid., 271.

45. Ibid., 229.

46. Lacan, *Seminar II,* 223.

47. Lacan, *The Four Fundamental Concepts,* 18.

48. W. Richardson, "Psychoanalysis and the Being-Question," in *Interpreting Lacan,* ed. J. Smith and W. Kerrigan, vol. 6, *Psychiatry and the Humanities* (New Haven: Yale University Press, 1983), 142.

49. W. Richardson (1983), "Lacan and the Subject of Psychoanalysis," in *Interpreting Lacan,* 51–74.

50. Ibid., 72.

51. Ibid., 73.

52. W. Richardson, "Psychoanalysis and the Being-Question," 149.

53. Some would argue the unconscious and sexuality, for example, Laplanche, *New Foundations in Psychoanalysis,* 59; J. Mitchell, "Freud and Lacan: Psychoanalytic Theories of Sexual Difference in Women," in *The Longest Revolution* (London: Virago, 1974), p. 250.

54. See Lemaire, *Jacques Lacan,* ch. 9; Laplanche *New Foundations in Psychoanalysis.*

55. S. Freud (1925[1924]), "A Note Upon the 'Mystic Writing-Pad'," *S.E.* 19: 227–34.

56. J. Lacan (1970) in Lemaire, *Jacques Lacan,* 118.

57. Ragland-Sullivan, *Jacques Lacan,* 53.

58. Ibid., 113.

59. Ibid., 113.

Index

Abraham, K., 56, 109, 115
Adaptation, 98–99
Adler, A., 84
Agency, 4, 5, 15, 53; in Anna Freud, 92; in dreams, 46–47; in Hartmann, 96–98; in Klein, 106–9; in Lacan, 132–40; in repression 52, 57, 62
Aggression, 113, 115
Alienation, 123
Amiel, H. F., 1
Anna O, 17
Antithetic ideas, 15–16, 17
Anxiety, 56, 62, 80, 106, 107
Archer, M., 155

Bär, E., 130
Bettleheim, B., 8–9, 35, 61, 78–79, 81
Biology, 53, 57, 101, 103
Bloch, E., 154
Bonaparte, M., 27, 28
Breuer, J., 17–18, 27

Castration, 159
Catharsis, 13, 48, 49
Cathexis, 18, 52, 60, 66, 75–76, 80, 116
Censorship, 19, 44–47, 50, 65, 68–69
Charcot, J. M., 14
Chepko, D. von, 139
Christian tradition, 157–58
Common sense, 14, 17, 54, 74, 85, 96, 102
Condensation, 45

Conflict-free ego sphere, 95–96
Conscious, 19, 61, 63, 64
Consciousness, 31, 38, 45, 51, 53, 56, 61, 67, 74, 80
Correspondence theory, 161–65
Counter-will, 15–16, 81

Death instinct, 59
Defense, 22, 34, 39, 92; in Anna Freud, 91–92; and intentionality, 19–21; and will, 17–18
Deferred action, 22, 34
Demand, 124
Denial, 91, 124
Depressive position, 115
Desire, 121, 124, 160, 171, 177
Disavowal, 83
Displacement, 22, 95
Double discourse, 4, 174–76
Dreams: *The Interpretation of Dreams*, 42–53; metapsychology of, 67–68; punishment, 51–52
Dual structure, 153–55

Ego, 19, 20, 38, 55, 58, 69; as agent of repression, 20, 22, 51, 52, 57, 71, 82; in Anna Freud, 91–92; of dreamer, 49; fate of, 80–82; in Hartmann, 95–99; instincts, 57–58; in Lacan, 125–31; in "Project," 32–34; restrictions of, 80; of second topography, 74–77; splitting of, 82–83; as subject and object, 36, 82;

Will, 34, 75, 81, 172–73; and defense,
 18–21; of *hystérique d'occasion* 13–21; in
 Hartmann, 97–99; in Rank, 84–85
Wish: in "Project," 32–34; in *Interpretation of Dreams,* 49–51; in punishment

dreams, 52; of pleasure-ego, 55
Wollheim, R., 31

Žižek, S., 141–44